D0857545

SAWDUST IN THEIR BLOOD

100 Years of the Hedstrom Lumber Co.

By Jim Boyd

North Shore Press
Grand Marais, Minn.

Photos provided by the Hedstrom Family and Maeri Hedstrom
Illustrations by Jeff Niesen
Book design by Amber Pratt
Cover design by Jim Nagy

U.S. Publisher

North Shore Press

Produced By

Northern Wilds Media, Inc.

103 W 1st PO Box 26

Grand Marais, MN 55604

(218) 387 9475

www.northernwilds.com

Copyright 2014

All Rights Reserved

ISBN 978-0-9740207-4-7

Printed in the United States of America by Bang Printing

10 9 8 7 6 5 4 3 2

FROM FOREST TO FINISHED PRODUCT

ANDREW HEDSTROM and SONS, Inc.

Grand Marais, Minnesota

Dedicated to the perseverance
of Andrew Hedstrom.

LARGEST STOCK of LUMBER on the NORTH SHORE

An artist's rendering of the mill
site and the family homestead.
Illustration by Jeff Niesen.

Contents

Introduction

This book tells the story of the business that my grandfather Andrew Hedstrom started 100 years ago. I believe author Jim Boyd had fun researching and writing this history. He found old writings and news articles, and conducted interviews that pulled together a picture of what it took for my grandfather to emigrate from his homeland to a new country, learn a new language, and cope with economic conditions that weren't much better than what he left in Sweden. Growing up in the family and business, you might think I know all about our history. Actually, reading this book taught me many things I didn't know. I hope you find it interesting and informative, too. It speaks to the hardships faced by pioneers, and how hard work and determination can overcome difficult odds.

The company started out logging and sawing lumber in remote winter camps, because all transportation was done by horses. In 1948, the mill was set up close to where it is now located. With the development of better roads, trucks could haul logs from farther distances. As the years progressed, the company was able to haul logs from greater distances. Our niche is sawing larger timber, and we are one of the few remaining mills in Minnesota to do so.

Our state is blessed with a wealth of forest land, including millions of acres of publicly owned forests managed by the U.S. Forest Service (national forests), the Minnesota Department of Natural Resources (state forests) and county land departments (tax forfeit lands). The forests in Minnesota are getting older and larger on average, so the flow of the type of logs processed at our mill should be unending. Our company and others have done much work in making sure there is the budget and policy in place to sustainably manage our forests. The trees cut into logs for our mill are anywhere from 40 to 140 years old, and over that lifespan we ride the roller coaster of changes in the public attitude about timber management. We therefore have to weather changing market demand, cost pressures from fuel and energy costs and changing availability because of changing attitudes about managing our forests.

Sawmill work is just that...work. But not just work. Specific skills and experience are key to keeping a sawmill business running. The machinery has to be robust to handle the logs and lumber, yet needs to be designed and maintained to achieve precision accuracy. Saws and knives need to be continually sharpened and tuned to cut accurately in all types of conditions. All workers need to know lumber grades as they make the cutting and sorting decisions throughout the process. The only way to learn these skills is on the job.

There are hundreds of people who have helped the business be successful over these 100 years, and Jim Boyd called out a few key individuals in this book. Six brothers of the Anderson family were involved in the early years; Charles (married to Mildred Hedstrom), Victor, Emil, Oliver, Joe and Arthur all worked at the mill and several of their sons have followed suit. Earl Anderson (son of Emil) worked for 40 years before retiring.

It would not be possible to point out everyone who worked in the business and contributed to our success. I can only say thank you to all who have worked here.

Our current employees are shown in the book in photos, and list the years of service. I am proud and honored at the dedication shown by the length of service. Hard work, knowing their job, doing the extra that is necessary to keep a mill running, and working safely has allowed our mill to stay running where many others have gone by the wayside. I thank past and present employees for their contributions.

—Howard Hedstrom,
President of
Hedstrom Lumber Company

A very young Howard Hedstrom beside a company truck. The rope was tied to his belt loop so he couldn't wander off.

Hedstrom

FRONT: Phil, Frances, Art, Andrew, Alma, Wes, Herb, Helen.
REAR: Carl, Roy, Lucille, Lawrence, Mildred, Andy.

Andrew Hedstrom
1870-1959

Alma Berglund
1879-1966

Frances 1899-1998
Married Alfred Fenstad

CAROL	ELIZABETH	MARSHALL	
M: Tom Eckel	M: C.A. E Johnson	M: Jean Bosley	
Mary Beth	Cary Lea	Michael	Bernard
Scott	Diane	Duncan	Juliet
David	Leslie Ann	Tessa	

Lawrence 1901-1998
Married Florence Tomkins

CARLYLE	ROBERT	HELEN MARGARET	⊢ PATRICIA ⊣		⊢ELIZABETH ANN⊣	
M: Virginia	M: Peggy	M: Bob Newall	M: Charles Landman	M: Pat Nacey	M: Robert Bidinger	M: Cyril Southwell
Carol	Robert	Katherine	Colleen	Shawn	Jonathan	
	Penny	Patricia	Katherine	Charles	Beth	
	Scott	Steven	Kelly			

Family Tree

Mildred 1903-1999
Married Charles Anderson

PHYLLIS		CHARLES		WAYNE
M: Bruce Gordon	M: Ken Bauer	M: Dorothy Martin	M: Carol Chrystal	M: Philis Blood
Alice Ann		Charles		Mark Matthew
		Stephen		Rolf Kent

Lucille 1905-1989
Married A.B. Walker

Roy 1907-1997
Married Sophia Olson

Alice 1909-1909

Helen 1910-1998
Married Gerald Kruse

KENNETH	PHIL	
	M: Lynne Yeatman	M: Pat Backes
	Shelly	
	Stefanie Steven	

Carl 1912-1979
Married Evelyn Hagger

BARBARA WALSTROM	KAREN WALSTROM	DAVID WALSTROM
M: Gene Erickson	M: Roger Seim	M: Gail Linnell
Khristi Elizabeth	Carey	Paige
Michael	Peter	Galen

W. Andrew 1915-1981
Married Hildur Bard

TOM	JACK	HOWARD	ANN		
	M: Gail Alden	M: Bonnie Gay Podas	M: Bob Bartz	M: Mike Foster	M: Ken M.
	Glen	Elizabeth	David	Franklin	
		Jonathan	Justin	Shelley	
		Maeri	Emily		

Herbert 1917-
Married Jane Tonkin

MARY JANE	MARGARET	ALAN	
Ron Soderberg	M: Robert Frost	M: Sue Olmscheid Bauer	M: Lynn Abrahamson
Justin		Milan	
		Amelia	

Arthur 1919-
Married Marian Robinson

DIANE	DEAN
M: Erick Wesman	M: Kristi Hawkinson
Christopher	M: Sandy Jacobsen
Jennifer	

Philip 1921-1994
Married Ruth Newman

STAN	ED	RUTHANNE
M: Jane Lind	M: Kris Kastner	M: Jim Vos
Tessa	Sam	Stephanie
Carly	Karel	Allison

Wesley 1924-2003
Married Thelma Berge

LINDA	JEANNE	ROBERT
M: Steve Noble	M: Doug Anderson	M: Mary Sanderlin
Andrew	M: Ed Finnegan	Olivia
Heather		Leon

ANDREW HEDSTROM'S JOURNEY

The winter of 1893-94 surely was a period of deep discontent for Andrew Hedstrom. This young, restlessly energetic man wasn't finding America the land of opportunity he'd expected, at least not yet.

Andrew left Sweden at age 21, on May 1, 1891, headed for Osage, Kansas, where his sister Hilma already lived. When he arrived in late May, he found work for the summer as a mason and plasterer working on bridge abutments. That winter, he shifted to working in a coal mine, but, "He didn't like it much," said grandson Wayne Anderson. "It was a narrow seam, and he had to lay on his side to pick at the coal. He decided that wasn't the work for him."

The original home of Andrew and Alma on Maple Hill, which was built by Andrew (shown).

In search of more pleasant opportunities, Andrew left Kansas for Duluth in April 1892, where he joined another sister, Anna, and her family. "Andrew immediately became acquainted with 14-year-old Alma Berglund, for he lived with his sister's family in the duplex house that Alma's father had built," reports Willis Raff in "Pioneers in the Wilderness." Andrew also began a carpentry partnership with Olaf Berglund, Alma's father, that was to last many years.

Andrew's prospects were looking up. He wrote his parents that, "I am working every day, and I like it here in Duluth—and feel that I am much better off than I was in Sweden."

Andrew was even thinking of college, he told his parents. "I had thought if I can save a little, I could go to school this winter," he wrote them. "I am thinking of going to St. Peter, a town that lies a little distance southwest of St. Paul. I think you have read in the newspaper about Gustave Adolph's College in St. Peter. If I can manage to make enough so I can attend school, it is well to get an education while I am still young...."

Through the summer and fall of 1892, Andrew worked steadily as a carpenter in Duluth and on the Iron Range. That winter, however, the Panic of 1893 put the economy into the worst depression the United States had yet seen, and work dried up as if someone had turned a tap. Unable to find employment in Duluth, Andrew traveled back to the Iron Range in the spring of 1893 but found no joy there, either. So it was once more to Duluth, where he eventually did get a job with a sash-and-door factory for the summer.

In 1892, Andrew had joined a number of Duluth's Swedish immigrants in filing the paperwork for 160-acre homesteads available in the western reaches of Maple Hill Township. The homesteads ran west from Meridian Road, just north of present-day County Road 6, in this order: Eric Gustaf Soderberg, Olaf Berglund, Andrew Backlund, Peter Backlund (husband of Andrew's sister Anna) and Andrew. His homestead must have been near what is known today as Blueberry Lake.

So in August 1893, Andrew came to Grand Marais for his first visit to his 160 acres. He was not impressed. The land lay four miles from the nearest road and was covered by rock and trees. One look at it, Andrew said years later, and he "decided not to come back."

With one more avenue to prosperity seemingly closed to him, Andrew returned to Duluth with the idea of collecting money he was owed and going to college. But with the national economy still in the pits, he couldn't collect, so any thought of school was out.

With no work at hand in Duluth, Andrew retreated to Grand Marais and his homestead, where he built a small cabin. Over the winter, he worked doing chores at The Lakeview Hotel in Grand Marais .

No real work to be had anywhere, a homestead in the middle of nowhere that looked anything but promising, and a North Shore winter: Had Andrew been given to pessimism, he would have packed it in. But he persevered. He apparently had an abundance of the tenacity and ability to adapt that characterized immigrants who carved out successful lives in the Northwoods.

That fall, Andrew wrote his parents, "I have also thought some of returning to Sweden, but by now I have overcome the hardest trials of an immigrant, and if I leave here now, I will have nothing for all my efforts. So I shall just stay here and wait for better times." It must have been a long and dispiriting winter, waiting for those better times.

But for this young Swede, waiting did not mean sitting on his hands. The next spring, 1894, he made his way back to the Iron Range and found temporary work as a carpenter at an iron mine. When the job ended, it was back to Duluth, where he found work at the same sash factory he had worked for the previous year. That work lasted into the fall.

Meanwhile, Olaf and his son Axel traveled to Grand Marais and spent the spring and summer of 1894 building a house on the Berglund homestead, three-quarters of a mile east of the Hedstrom homestead.

That fall, Axel brought the entire family back to the homestead. Alma came with them but lived separately: She had contracted to be the first teacher for Maple Hill, which required living near the school, which, that first year, was in the Hans Gilbertsen home in the central Maple Hill community (near where the cemetery and church now are located). Alma lived in a small log cabin on Dave Caribou's homestead, along with Axel, who attended school as one of her students.

Also that fall, Andrew returned to his homestead for

Andrew Hedstrom

"He was a very ingenious man. He was a carpenter; he learned the carpenter trade in Sweden, but he was more than a carpenter. He was very resourceful, and when he came up here, he built their house up on Maple Hill. Pictures of it exist. It was a beautiful house, all hewn logs, handmade siding and shingles, and ornamental work like they did on railings. He did it all by himself in the wintertime when he couldn't do anything else.

"He worked as a carpenter in town, built quite a few buildings.... He made a cement mixer that he ran with a horse, a blind horse. And it didn't look like cement mixers look nowadays. It was a rectangular box, with a lid on it, and a shaft ran through one corner of the box and out the other corner, so when it turned the stuff tumbled from one end to the other. It had a lid, and they would shovel it full of gravel and cement and pour in water, close the lid, and the horse would go, and when it was done they'd dump the cement. He built a lot of stuff with that, bridges and many things. That was THE cement mixer in town.

"He was fiery, I guess is the way to say it, and impatient, everything had to happen right now. He never walked, he ran. He had a very volatile temper but it would only last a minute and then he would be right back to what he'd been doing. There's many, many stories about him that may or may not be true. They're all funny.

"One of them was that when he had the sawmill, before forklifts, they had a log deck inclined toward the mill. They'd skid the logs up with a horse and roll them onto this deck with a cant hook. Apparently one got away and was rolling down the deck. He went after it and grabbed it with a cant hook, which is something you do not do. You get in front of them on the corner and try to hold them, but you don't run after them, and you can figure out why. Well of course it launched him through the air, and he went flying. A local guy, Adolph Everson, told me the story, he was there; so Grandpa Hedstrom got up; he was mad as a wet hen of course, but he didn't get hurt. He told the crew, 'I don't care what you do, but I quit. I'm going home.' So he went home, and a few minutes later he was back, and they went back to work, and that was it.

"He was very outspoken; if there was something to be said, he would say it, whether it should be said or not. But the thing is he had a way about him that everyone accepted that and it didn't make anyone mad.

"There's a story, and I don't know if it's true, that's another of Adolph Everson's stories, that he (Andrew) was putting a glass in a French door or something with a lot of panes in it, and as he was putting it in, he broke the glass, and he took the hammer and went down the door and went plunk, plunk, plunk, plunk, broke all the panes. Then he put them all back in."

—Wayne Anderson

the winter, four miles from Alma. In her excellent booklet celebrating the 90th anniversary of Hedstrom Lumber Co., writer Elizabeth Hillstrom sets the scene:

"Andrew Hedstrom didn't mind a long walk in the winter. He would travel for miles, navigating snowdrifts as winds, wild and unsympathetic, buried the trails. Although his layers of wool were thick and well-fastened, they often proved weaker than the weather. But Andrew was unwaver-

ing and well-traveled by the age of 24, and he was hardly discouraged by a tempestuous winter day. Besides, he didn't want to keep his future bride waiting too long between visits, and even in harsh conditions, Andrew regularly made the four-mile trip from his home to hers.

"During her first winter on Maple Hill in 1894, Alma Berglund frequently looked through the small window in her log cabin. Often the 16-year-old, who was Maple Hill's

The Berglund family. **From lower left:** Alma, Annie and Alfred. **From top left:** Judith, Axel, Adeline and Mabel.

first schoolteacher, could see Andrew approaching, knowing that the few miles he traveled to see her were hardly arduous compared to the thousands he journeyed before settling on Maple Hill."

In the late summer and fall of 1894, Andrew also found time to get involved in Cook County politics. By then, he'd made the acquaintance of Chris Murphy, editor of the Cook County Herald, whose home Andrew and Olaf would build in 1896. Murphy, a Democrat, was involved in an acrimonious feud with Republican old-timers like Henry Mayhew who controlled the county board. This came during the short ascendance of the national People's Party, which viewed both Republicans and Democrats as controlled by banks, railroads and wealthy Eastern elites.

In "Pioneers in the Wilderness," Willis Raff reports, "Acting on Murphy's initiative, a group of men held a meeting in the office of the Herald in late August and organized themselves as the People's Party of Cook County. Seeking to associate themselves formally with the state party, they chose delegates to the forthcoming People's Party District

Convention in Duluth; the delegates to be: Andrew Hedstrom, A.S. Carlson and Hans Holte."

Ultimately, however, the People's Party rebellion came to nought.

The following spring of 1895, Andrew, still doing whatever it took to get ahead, secured a job prospecting with "Nickel" Frank Johnson. In 1955, for a News-Herald article by county historian Olga Soderberg, Andrew recalled, "The last part of April 1895, I went up with Nickel Johnson to Gaskin Lake.... The snow was all gone, and the lakes were open. They had started to sink a shaft between Gaskin and Winchell Lake the fall of 1894. We continued digging for awhile, then we were moved 300 or 400 feet northeast and started drilling and blasting for a while in, if I remember right, granite."

The prospecting produced nothing, and eventually Andrew was laid off. Whereupon he returned to Maple Hill and made what would prove to be an extraordinarily favorable agreement with Dave Caribou, Alma's landlord: Andrew agreed to build a log cabin for Caribou in return for 20 acres on central Maple Hill.

With Caribou's cabin completed and his 20 Maple Hill acres secure, Andrew joined forces that fall with Olaf to build a log home for editor Chris Murphy in Grand Marais. The two men felled the timber about two miles east of Grand Marais and arranged to have the logs dragged to town during the winter so that construction could begin the following summer.

Also that fall, Olaf and Andrew contracted to build a house for the Grand Marais lighthouse keeper. Their craftsmanship still can be appreciated: The house now is the museum for the Cook County Historical Society.

Thus did Andrew put together one building job here, one road construction job there, to create the beginnings of a prosperous life in Grand Marais.

One fall day in 1897—no one appears to know which day—Andrew took his fate in hand and asked Alma to be his wife. That she said yes is most apparent in the historical record of Andrew's frenetic activity that fall and winter: He returned to the 20 acres on central Maple Hill acquired from Dave Caribou and began clearing the land for a home. "I worked all that fall and winter," Andrew recalled later, "cut and hewed logs, sawed lumber with a whipsaw, made a rig for splitting shingles from cedar blocks, dug a cellar and erected a four-room house with space for rooms upstairs. I had the roof on and windows in by spring. I then started to clear land for a garden and some potatoes." The home he fashioned was beautiful, sophisticated and filled with artistic carpentry.

On Aug. 6, 1898, Andrew and Alma took the steamer Dixon to Duluth and were married. They made some household purchases and returned to Maple Hill to begin their marriage and their family.

In that era, it was taken for granted that Alma's teaching career ended with her marriage. Teaching frequently was something a woman did between finishing school and starting a family. Alma came back into education to serve as first superintendent of schools for Cook County from 1903 to 1906, but her main occupation from 1898 on was keeping house and tending a growing family. And did it grow: Alma bore Andrew a child every two or three years for a quarter of a century: Frances was the first to arrive, in 1899, followed

Olaf Hedstrom, Andrew's father, built spinning wheels in Sweden. Circa 1870.

by Lawrence in 1901, Mildred in 1903, Lucille in 1905, Roy in 1907, Alice in 1909 (she lived only a month), Helen in 1910, Carl in 1912, Andy in 1915, Herb in 1917, Art in 1919, Phil in 1921 and Wes in 1924.

From 1898 to 1913, life on Maple Hill settled into a routine. Andrew and Olaf worked together on many building projects, and Andrew did a number on his own. Almost all building materials, including most lumber, had to be brought to Grand Marais by boat; it was expensive, seasonal and somewhat unreliable, factors that eventually influenced Andrew's decision to get into the sawmill business.

Logging and lumbering were just arriving in Cook County at the beginning of the 20th century, more than 50 years after they became a central focus of economic activity in other parts of Minnesota. There were various reasons for this late focus on trees and their economic potential. Early exploration of the area had focused almost exclusively on the hunt for valuable mineral deposits. Plus, the almost total lack of roads, both local and connecting to the larger world via Duluth, made all but the smallest timber projects impractical. Indeed, the first large logging operations focused exclusively on timber close by the shore of Lake Superior, which could be used to float logs to sawmills located elsewhere. The John Schroeder Lumber Co., for example, bought up timber rights on 23,000 acres in the Cross River drainage in 1895. The river itself was the vehicle used to get the logs to the Big Lake, where they were rafted up and towed to Schroeder mills in Wisconsin.

Andrew got into logging and, eventually, lumbering through what, looking back, seems a supreme irony: It all came about because of fire. And fire would play a recurring, dramatic role in the saga of the Hedstrom clan and Hedstrom Lumber Co. for the next century.

The years 1908 through 1910 were horrible forest fire years in the North Woods. The summers were uncommonly dry, and the invasion of the forests by Europeans and their fire-inducing mechanisms—for mining, logging, fishing, hunting, road building—caused the fire danger to soar. In addition, logging operations weren't at all hygienic: The slash they generated was simply left, elevating the fire danger still further. Fires in 1910 produced such horror—including the October Baudette Fire which killed 43 people—that in 1911, the Minnesota Legislature established the office of state forester, whose first job it was to ensure that logging companies appropriately disposed of the slash that logging operations left behind.

The fire of 1908 that almost destroyed Grand Marais is well-known and documented. The fires that September extended from Grand Rapids to Thunder Bay. A less-known fire in 1910 did destroy most of Tofte. The Grand Forks Daily Herald reported on May 11, 1910, that "only eight buildings" were left standing. One of the buildings destroyed housed the Tofte Mill Co. sawmill, owned by Ed Toftey.

Shortly after the 1910 fire, Toftey relocated his family to Grand Marais and opened a store. It's not difficult to imagine a conversation sometime in 1913 between Ed Toftey and Andrew concerning a burned-out sawmill for sale in Tofte. However it happened, Andrew found himself the new owner of an old sawmill.

The mill was a disaster. After burning in 1910, it had sat out in the elements for three years. The shafts had been badly bent by the fire, all of the bearings had melted, the boiler was burnt out, and everything was covered in rust. The common conclusion was that Andrew had bought several tons of junk that could never again be made to function as a working sawmill. But Andrew was determined, and he had the help of an exceptionally skillful mechanic, Charles Anderson.

By this time, Andrew was 43 years old and had a couple of decades under his belt as a Cook County carpenter. Charles Anderson was just 27. He and Andrew had worked together on a number of projects already, and Charles eventually would marry Andrew's daughter Mildred.

"My grandpa Andrew never worked alone," Charles' son Wayne explained. "He always had a helper, so because my dad was living on the hill here and he was available, Andrew would hire him. They did many, many things before Andrew started the sawmill.... They drilled a well up on Maple Hill by hand with a birch spring pole.... They also hilled potatoes by hand. My grandpa made some sort of a shovel plow, and Grandpa pulled and my dad pushed, and they hilled potatoes that way. That's the kind of guy Andrew Hedstrom was. He did a lot of things, but he always liked to have help, so that's how that came about."

Great-grandson Kent Anderson, who is not only Wayne's son but also an avid woodsman and logger, said it was Andrew's carpentry that piqued his interest in logging the fire-damaged timber: He needed lumber.

"That would go back to all the building, the lumber he was using," Kent said.

Wayne agreed: "A fire prior to that, I think it was the fire of 1910, there were a lot of big fires about then. And so there was a lot of burned timber available. And he used to do some logging. So he logged some timber. And he had—I can't remember his first name; they called him "Old Man Creech—he had a local mill here, probably been in 1912 or '13. Anyhow, he (Andrew) would log, and he'd have Creech saw the lumber for him. And I guess that sort of introduced him to the value of sawmilling. Then when this Toftey mill out in Tofte became available, he bought it.... It was a mill that had burned. And then they moved it in the wintertime on horses and sleighs and brought it to Grand Marais."

"When I think about this I marvel," Wayne continued. "How would you have liked to be the guy who was sent out

Alma Hedstrom
(Berglund)

"Mamma was a beautiful woman, tall and stately, with big brown eyes, a clear complexion and long dark brown hair. One of my vivid memories is watching her comb her hair. She would bend over from her waist and comb from the nape of her neck up over the back of her head. When it was smooth she twisted her hair into a bun on the crown of her head, which she fastened with several bone hair pins, relaxing the hair around her face so it resembled a halo, instead of pulling it tight, as so many women did.

"She was mild-tempered and soft-spoken, and seldom nagged, but when reprimanding was necessary, we knew she meant it. Many times a stern look was all that was needed. Spankings were few and far between."

"From the beginning our home was open to anyone and everyone's neighbors, friends, ministers, traveling 'would-be missionaries' and whomever happened by. Whenever there were services at the Maple Hill Church, the minister was always a guest at Sunday dinner."

"Mamma was county superintendent of schools for a term, about 1904-1906. I remember her driving off with the horse and buggy to visit the schools at Maple Hill, Colville and Good Harbor Hill. But I have wondered how she got to Hovland, Lutsen, Tofte and Schroeder.

"Whenever a new baby was born in the neighborhood, Mamma would pay the new mother a visit and bring fruit soup, which she carried in a two-quart syrup pail. She must have seemed like an angel of mercy to some mothers, whose husbands, though they earned some money doing road work, would spend their pay at the saloon before going home in a bad mood to sleep off their stupor."

"There were of course no modern conveniences, so washing clothes was done by heating water in a copper boiler on the kitchen stove, then dipping it into washtubs, where the clothes were scrubbed on a washboard, then rinsed twice. We

did have a handwringer. The white clothes, sheets, pillowcases, shirts and towels, were bailed in soapy water after rubbing, then rinsed. In winter, as in summer, clothes were hung outside to dry. We often had to wade through deep snow to get to the clotheslines. The clothes froze hard immediately, and we had to pin them on securely to keep them from blowing away in the wind. It was often two or three days before they could be taken in to finish inside. Laundry was a long, hard day's work, starting early in the morning and finishing in the late afternoon."

"As the seasons came and went, there was planting, weeding, hoeing potatoes, haying and harvesting. There was no bakery close by so we baked all the bread, cakes and cookies. Early summer was the time to can rhubarb, then pick wild raspberries and blueberries and can them for our winter's supply of fruit.

"On one of the last boats in the fall, Mamma and Papa would lay in a supply of staple groceries to last until the first boat in the spring. There would be several 100 lb. bags of white flour, a bag or two of rye flour, cornmeal, oatmeal, two or three 100-lb. bags of sugar, brown sugar, beans, coffee, prunes, raisins, dried apples, a tub of lard and a barrel or two of apples."

Mamma's profound faith in God, her love of nature and her family surely helped to sustain her health and sanity during the hardest times when epidemics of measles, scarlet fever, whooping cough and colds swept through the whole family. Baby Alice died of whooping cough when she was 6 weeks old. This was a very traumatic time for all of us. I was 10 years old, so I remember it well. Papa and Grandpa Berglund built the little coffin and Grandma Berglund came over and helped Mamma line it with white muslin. The funeral was held in our front room, and the house was filled to capacity with families and neighbors...."

—Frances (Hedstrom) Fenstad

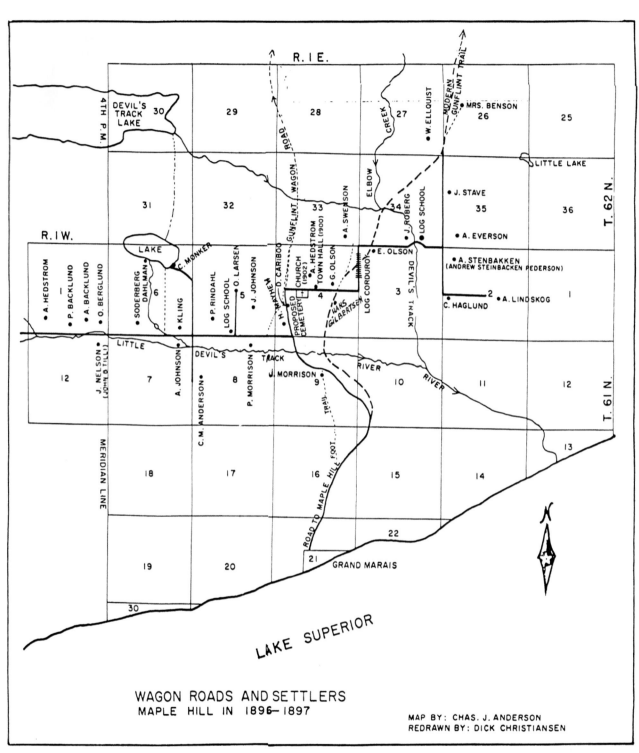

WAGON ROADS AND SETTLERS
MAPLE HILL IN 1896-1897

MAP BY: CHAS. J. ANDERSON
REDRAWN BY: DICK CHRISTIANSEN

The map above shows the locations of the original homesteads on Maple Hill. Andrew Hedstrom's homestead is on the far left, north of the Little Devil Track River.

Reprinted from Pioneers in the Wilderness, by William Raff. Reprinted with permission from the Cook County Historical Society.

there with horses, and you've somehow got to load a steam engine which weighed tons and a boiler which weighed tons and the sawmill? They must have had to make more than one trip.... Nowadays, you'd get ahold of Thoreson and have the crane there, but they had to do it with horses and by hand, with blocks and rollers and screw jacks. It was a feat, I'm sure. But anyhow, they got it here, and in the spring they started working on it. That was primarily my dad and Andrew who did the millwrighting work."

"When a mill is burnt," Kent added, "especially in those days, you know, they did not have ball bearings and shafts like what we have for modern mills. It was all babbitt." A babbitt is a solid bearing made of soft metal embedded with particles of very hard metal to slow the wear.

Wayne: "And all the babbitt had melted and run out. It was stuck; everything was stuck, and even the boiler was all burnt out."

"My grandpa hired a wood builder to build the building," Wayne said, "a two-story mill building, heavy enough that the mill ran on the second floor, and everything dropped down. There were no elevating conveyors and stuff like you have nowadays when you have electricity. Everything had to fall by gravity. As the slabs and what developed, they were cut up into lengths and dropped into a dump cart pulled by a horse. They had an overhead tramway that the lumber went out on so they could pull it off and pile it.

"But anyhow, to get this steam engine and boiler and all working, to get it loose and get the rust taken off and rebabbitted—even the line shafts were crooked, and they had to hammer them with sledgehammers and roll them to try to get them straight. I know when they poured the babbitt boxes on the steam engine—they were huge—they didn't have any babbitt pot big enough so they heated babbitt in a big frying pan in the forge and poured with that.

"All the time they were working on this, the building contractor, Louie Falk his name was, he'd be watching out of the corner of his eye, and he'd say, 'It's never gonna run; that will never run.' They were working basically with junk. You can imagine: No way to drill; no way to grind or sand; everything either had to be done with a file or sandpaper or something. If you had to make a hole in something, you had to heat it red hot in the forge and then punch a hole in it. No welding, no acetylene torch, nothing but a few hand tools. When they got it running, this Falk, he could hardly believe

it. It worked! According to the record, they sawed 10,000 board feet the first day, which is remarkable; that's a lot of lumber for a single-saw mill."

The date was July 14, 1914, and Andrew was well and truly in the sawmill business, on a site south of the Devil Track river, in the triangle of land bounded by the Gunflint Trail, County Road 60 and the Devil Track—across the river from where the current mill is located.

HUMBLE BEGINNINGS

By 1914, Andrew had established himself as a respected carpenter and craftsman in Cook County. But when he and Charles Anderson powered up their steam mill on July 14 and prepared for their first day of cutting lumber, could he possibly have imagined that he was setting in motion a way of life that would define the Hedstrom family, and play an oversized role in the life of the county, for at least the next century? Did he have any sense of how momentous were the consequences of starting the steam-driven saw on its first rotation?

The original steam mill looking east from County Road 60. The white house in the center of the photograph was the family home that burned in 1923.

The original steam mill was in operation until it burned down in 1929.

Art looking east from the Devil Track River bridge on County Road 60 at the steam mill.

Perhaps he actually did. It is a testament to his vision, and his bravery, that even before the "pile of junk" mill had left Tofte, let alone undergone the Herculean effort needed to make it work, Andrew had begun construction on not only the machine shed needed to get the mill working, but also the bunkhouse and cook house and barn that a functioning sawmill would require. And during the winter of 1913-14, Andrew also put a logging crew to work filling the new log yard with the first pine logs the sawmill would process.

Andrew literally bet everything on the mill. Now there was no time to undertake carpentry projects in town, so that income stream dried up. Meanwhile, the investment in the buildings, sleds, wagons, horses, saws, axes, harness and other equipment severely strained his available resources.

Even after the mill had proven itself, the Hedstroms scraped by, though they never went hungry or without clothing and shelter. Writing in her very personal family history booklet, "And the Lord God Watched Over Them," Frances (Hedstrom) Fenstad talked of her effort to become a teacher: "I was so anxious to help out financially as much as possible, as Papa was still struggling to make ends meet, and there was never anything for extras. By doing that it took me five years to finish a two-year course for a teacher's diploma."

The winter of 1913-14, and for several winters after, most logging focused on Section 36, Township 62, 1 East, which translates into the 640 acres immediately northeast of the present-day intersection of Lindskog Road and County Road 60. Section 36 of every township was designated the "school section," so whatever Andrew paid for the timber most likely would have gone into a fund to support area schools.

From the beginning, the Hedstrom enterprise wasn't just a sawmill; it was a logging concern as well. Hedstrom crews cut and trimmed the trees, skidded them to loading areas with horses, hauled them to the mill on sleds, sawed them into lumber, stacked and air-dried the lumber and then sold it—some locally, most hauled to Grand Marais for shipment by boat to Duluth. Later, a planing mill was added, so that the dried lumber could be made smooth and true. A kiln, where the lumber was heated and dried quickly, was decades away.

At first, the work done by Hedstrom crews was seasonal. In the fall, preparations were made for the winter logging: timber identified, roads created, equipment readied, plans drawn. The actual logging, skidding logs to loading areas and hauling the logs to the mill occupied crews all winter. Unlike logging crews in other parts of Minnesota, Andrew had no rivers or railroads to move logs around. His crews had only horses, so they took maximum advantage of northeastern Minnesota's snow and ice, which made it enormously easier—though still no picnic—for horses to both drag fallen logs to a loading area and haul sleds piled with tremendous loads to the mill. Plus, in winter there was much less trouble negotiating wetlands and bogs.

But snow and ice were not helpful when it came to getting logs and lumber to the Grand Marais dock for transport to Duluth. Howard Hedstrom, current president of Hedstrom Lumber Co., and Andrew's grandson, tells of men running alongside the sleds coming down the grade into Grand Marais. Their job was to throw straw under the runners in an effort to slow a sled's progress. Sometimes it worked, and sometimes it didn't. If the sled got away, Howard said, the drivers would bail off, and the sled would careen down the hill to crash at the bottom, inevitably killing the team of horses. "They lost quite a few horses that way," Howard said.

In the spring, the logging would end, and the sawing would commence, running until late summer. That first year, 1914, the Hedstrom mill ran from July 14 through August. A short note in the Cook County News-Herald from Sept. 3, 1914, records that, "The Hedstrom sawmill on Maple Hill, having completed a cut of about 400,000 feet of lumber, has closed down for the season."

Andrew working at a portable mill.

Andrew's Close Call

Early last week, Andrew Hedstrom narrowly escaped a horrible death at his sawmill on Maple Hill. While busying himself about the mill his clothes were caught in an exposed set-screw on a shaft and in a twinkling he was stripped of every stitch of clothing except his shoes and the sleeves and neck band of his undershirt. The fact that his clothes were not of a strong fabric was all that saved him from instant death. As it was, his only injury was a slightly strained leg by which he was laid up for a couple of days. When the engineer got a glimpse of clothes winding on the shaft he stopped the machinery instantly, and his relief can well be imagined when he went there and found Mr. Hedstrom, though stark naked, apparently unhurt. As was then remarked by the engineer, Mr. Hedstrom must certainly have a charmed life. This was his second miraculous escape within a year. It will be remembered that about a year ago he was caught under a falling building and was pinned so tight to the ground that he could not move, and was held there for many minutes that must have seemed like days to him, while excited men worked to pry the building up, expecting to find him crushed to pulp. And when the building was raised sufficiently he crawled out without assistance, his only injuries being a few insignificant scratches about his face and head.

From an undated clipping taken from the Cook County News-Herald, circa 1915

Roy standing by the company's Huffman truck in the early 1920s.

McCormick-Deering tractor with logs from Little Lake, circa 1928.

Meanwhile, the advent of the sawmill meant dramatic changes for Alma as well. The mill was two miles from the Hedstrom home, and Andrew frequently was required to make that journey on foot. He had to be at the mill at 5 a.m. to fire the boiler so the plant was ready to start producing at 7 a.m., and frequently did not leave work until after 5 p.m., so that two-mile distance was a significant hardship. Plus, he needed Alma close to the mill so she could oversee feeding the mill crew three meals each day.

So in 1915 (some accounts say 1916), Andrew built a new, smaller home a bit east of the sawmill and moved his family into it. Frances Fenstad recalled, "I never heard Mamma complain, but it must have wrenched her heart to leave that nice roomy home on the hill and learn to be content with less than one third of the space, and many times as much work—such as feeding 12-14 men three times a day. They ate first, and after cleaning the table

Logging Ice Roads

"Whenever a picture is shown of a large load of logs being hauled by a single- or four-horse team, the question usually asked is: 'How could those horses pull that large load of logs.'

"If the questioners knew the effort that was put into laying out and maintaining the ice roads for logging and into the construction of the sleighs, it would be easier to understand."

"Once it was decided that a certain stand of timber was to be cut, the first matter was the laying out of the logging road. The walking boss, or foreman, along with one of the timber cruisers, would lay out the road from the timber to the landing.... Sometimes the roads had to wind around considerably in order to find a level roadbed.

"Next came the job of cutting the logging road—starting usually in late September or October. Right-of-way was grubbed and leveled. In grubbing through standing timber, moss and dirt was removed from around the tree roots with a grub hoe, and the roots were cut off while the tree was still standing, so in falling the tree pulled the center root out and made the grubbing much easier....

"Water holes would be prepared in a creek or swamp adjoining the road by blasting with dynamite. Just as soon as freezing weather set in, the camp foreman would send out the water tanks and start preparing the road. If snow had fallen, all snow was removed so as to get the ice started right down to the soil. If good freezing weather prevailed, it would take about six weeks to get the ice road in shape for hauling....

"When the ice was ready, a 'rut cutter' was sent to make ruts for the sleigh runners. The rut cutter had blades that

Horse-drawn drays were used to haul logs and lumber.

cut parallel ruts about four inches deep....

"When the road was being built, the water tank crew worked all day and sometimes all night, but after the hauling began the tanks only worked nights when the log sleighs were off the road...."

"Where loads went down hills, hay or straw had to be placed in the ruts to keep the load from going too fast. A hay hill road was always dangerous, as sometimes frost would form on the hay and the load would start moving too fast and the horses would stumble and be injured.

"Most horse-drawn logging sleighs were 7 feet 4 inches between the runners.... Runners ... were made of oak, and companies usually had a lot of 4-inch-by-12-inch-by-8-foot oak planks sawed up in their mills

and sent to the camps for making runners. Runners on most sleighs were 7 feet long, and cast iron shoes were preferred to steel shoes as they would not get so hot from the friction of the road."

"When loads were spotted out for the night, they often had to have an extra team to get them started, after hitting each runner with a large wooden maul made for that purpose. But once they got underway it was surprising the load a four-horse team could haul over a well-constructed and maintained ice road."

—From Early Loggers in Minnesota by J.C. Ryan

A 1918 picture of the Hedstrom children and two friends. **From right:** Helen, Roy, Andy, Carl and Herb Hedstrom with friends Bernard and Alden.

and resetting, the family ate, often with extra guests. Water had to be carried from the creek up to the house, where it was poured into a large barrel and heated by pipes running through the firebox of the large [cook stove]. Besides cooking the meals, there was the never-ending baking of all the bread, pies, cakes, doughnuts and cookies. There were clothes to be washed and ironed, socks to be mended, and little ones to attend to. It was here Herbert, Art, Philip and Wesley were born. Lucille and Mildred were about 12 and 14 now, so they were a big help."

When available timber near the mill became scarce, the first remote logging camp was established in 1919, in the southeast quarter of Section 26, Township 62 North, 1 East. The camp was near Little Lake, east of the Gunflint Trail and the George Washington Pines. It was used until 1923-24. The Cook County News-Herald of Aug. 27, 1964, in its report on the 50th anniversary of the Hedstrom mill, says that W.C. Smith of Schroeder was camp foreman the first winter and that "Emil Anderson and Charley Bray, son of N.J. Bray, were among those employed building the camp."

A logging camp brought a great many changes to the operation: Men lived in and operated from the camp instead of walking to and from the logging site each morning. Meals were prepared in the camp itself, with lunch hauled to the loggers by horse and sled (soup, beans, sandwiches, pie, tea brewed from melted snow, oats and hay for the essential horses).

Meanwhile, in 1917, Andrew added a second mill, a shingle and lath mill. It lasted only a few years before demand for its products dried up, and it was replaced by a box mill to turn out fish boxes. Herb Hedstrom, now 96, recalls that one of his jobs as a youngster was banging fish boxes together. He much preferred that to his first chore, handling slabs, the barked outside pieces first cut from a log to square it. All of the boys, when they were 12 or 13, were expected to help at the mill in some capacity, whether taking care of the horses, handling slabs, making fish boxes or other chores. It also was a Hedstrom family ethic that as the boys reached maturity, if they wanted work in the mill, work would be found for them. Most of them indeed made the mill their careers. Meanwhile, the girls were expected to help Alma with the cooking, laundry, cleaning, canning, sewing and myriad other chores that went with keeping that half of the enterprise in good order.

The Hedstrom family barely escaped tragedy on a bitterly cold night in December 1922: In the wee hours, with the temperature at minus 20 and, as Frances wrote in her family history, "with a cellar full of canned fruit, potatoes (and) vegetables for the winter," the house caught fire and was totally destroyed. The family escaped and "found shelter in the bunkhouse a short distance away, with two double bunks in one room and a stove and table in the other," Frances writes. "This was a major calamity with seven children between ages 1 (and) 12, most of the food supply gone, and all of the clothes (destroyed) except their night wear."

"There was a storage room and woodshed," Frances continues, "near where the house had stood, which was converted into living quarters: a bedroom-living room on one side and kitchen-dining room on the other; a lean-to and cellar were added on for wood and storage. These two rooms became the nucleus of the permanent home as we know it now. It was enlarged little by little during the following six-eight years."

In August 1923, daughter Mildred married Charles Anderson, and that marked the end of Charles' millwright work. That winter, the couple moved to the logging camp in Section 26, where Mildred cooked for the loggers and Charles worked in the woods. Charles then joined the U.S. Forest Service for a short while before joining the Minnesota Forestry Department (which became the Department of Natural Resources). He remained with the DNR for the rest of his working life.

In Charles' departure is evidence that even after a decade of sawmill operations, the Hedstrom clan was barely making ends meet. Why did Charles leave? He was, after all, the mechanical wizard who restored a pile

of junk into a working sawmill. Charles' son Wayne says that while his grandfather and his dad always were on good terms, his dad didn't always get paid, and with a new family developing, he needed a job that consistently put groceries on the table. That was a sentiment Andrew well understood, not least because his daughter's well-being was involved.

In 1925-26, logging took the Hedstroms full circle: Their logging crew returned to central Maple Hill and logged the northeast quarter of Section 4, Township 61 North, 1 East. This was the area south of the old schoolhouse where Alma taught before her marriage.

Andrew added more new equipment in 1927: A small, portable mill used to cut lumber for the box mill. It also was hired out in the winter to cut birch ties in the Lutsen area for Hjalmer Helmerson.

Once again, however, that Hedstrom nemesis—fire—struck a brutal blow at the family enterprise: In March 1929, just as the mill was gearing up for the season, fire consumed the sawmill, the planing mill and box mill. They were a total loss, and none of it was covered by insurance. Despite all the years of hard work, the Hedstroms confronted the bleak prospect of starting over, again.

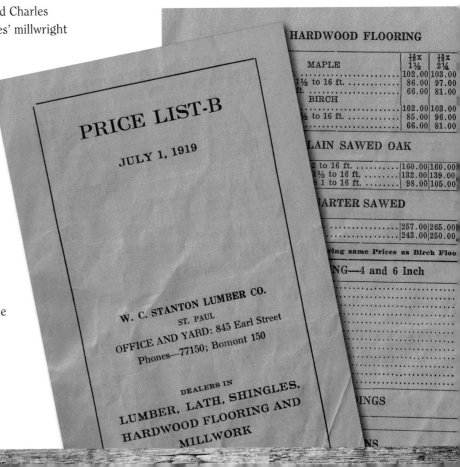

A 1919 price list from the W.C. Stanton Lumber Company in St. Paul shows lumber prices from that era.

PRICE LIST-B

JULY 1, 1919

W. C. STANTON LUMBER CO.
ST. PAUL
OFFICE AND YARD: 845 Earl Street
Phones—77150; Bomont 150

DEALERS IN
LUMBER, LATH, SHINGLES,
HARDWOOD FLOORING AND
MILLWORK

HARDWOOD FLOORING

	13/16 x 1½	13/16 x 2¼
MAPLE		
....	102.00	103.00
1½ to 16 ft.	86.00	97.00
ft.	66.00	81.00
BIRCH		
	102.00	103.00
½ to 16 ft.	85.00	96.00
....	66.00	81.00

PLAIN SAWED OAK

2 to 16 ft.	160.00	160.00
1½ to 16 ft.	132.00	139.00
1 to 16 ft.	98.00	105.00

QUARTER SAWED

| .... | 257.00 | 265.00 |
| .... | 243.00 | 250.00 |

ring same Prices as Birch Floo

NG—4 and 6 Inch

WINTERS IN THE WOODS

With his home place mill up in flames, Andrew set about creating a new and unusual dual-focus business. For rough sawing logs, he purchased an old McCormick-Deering tractor to run a single saw via a belt drive. This portable sawmill traveled with the loggers into the winter woods. Logs were rough sawn right there, then the lumber was transported to the home place where, gradually, a number of machines were added to refine the rough boards into finished products during the summer sawing season.

Fay McKeever skidding logs at a Hedstrom winter camp.

A sawmill set up at Hungry Jack Lake in 1942.

Operating a portable mill at a winter camp.

This was classic Hedstrom behavior. Again and again, during Andrew's life and after, the clan has shown itself to be extraordinarily nimble and adaptive. That's one big reason why Hedstrom Lumber Co. survived when so many others—including much larger enterprises with much deeper pockets—didn't: The family always has worked hard to make the most of whatever situation confronted it. The Hedstroms also have been willing to explore new ways of doing things that would improve their processes, increase efficiency, save on labor, squeeze a little more saleable product from each log and take advantage of any new, underserved market niche that presented itself. In the jargon of the computer age, they were early adopters.

Thus, the Hedstrom winter camps weren't just logging camps; they were logging and sawmill camps. This meant they were more elaborate affairs, requiring larger quarters for housing and feeding crews, accommodations for more horses and buildings to house the mill. As they came of age, all of the Hedstrom boys spent time working in the camps. Eventually the McCormick-Deering tractor got replaced by diesel-powered saws, which added to the complexity of constructing, maintaining and, every few years, moving this logging/sawmill operation.

Camp work, whether felling and skidding logs or cutting rough timber, was hard, grueling, dangerous, dirty work, outdoors in brutally cold weather. The Hedstroms became known for paying well and serving good food, but even those benefits didn't diminish by much the hardship that defined life in a northern Minnesota winter logging camp. Only at weekends, or occasionally at mid-week, were the workers carried to Grand Marais and reunited with their families.

At the home place, immediately following the '29 fire, a new building was put up to house a few small band saws, a single-surface planer and a resaw—all used to finish the rough lumber arriving from the woods. Then in 1930, Al Fenstad, husband of Frances, secured a 12-inch moulder from Hines Lumber Co. in Chicago, which greatly increased the Hedstroms' ability to turn out specialty products. In the history that Margaret wrote in 1964 on the 50th anniversary of the company's founding, she reported, "The freight from Chicago was as much as the cost of the machine." Gradually, from 1930 to 1935, this finishing mill was expanded and improved.

The fire in '29 couldn't have come at a more inopportune time; a few months later, the U.S. and then the world economies tanked, which dried up both financing for a new mill and markets for lumber. The Hedstroms scraped by, but as with many businesses, they did not do much more than survive until World War II came along. The war forced the federal government into what was essentially a massive Depression-ending stimulus program. Washington took on enormous debt to finance mobilization and production of the tools of war.

For the Hedstroms, the benefits came in the form of a revived shipbuilding sector in Duluth, which needed all the wood it could find, especially large timbers. Several shuttered shipyards reopened, and new ones were created. At the height of production, Twin Ports shipyards employed more than 10,000 men and women, and built an average of 10 ships per month.

Another beneficial result of the war boom was construction of the Hedstroms' first dry kiln in 1946. In keeping with the family culture of innovation, the kiln was an experimental type developed by the U.S. Forest Service's Forest Products Laboratory in Madison, Wis. The laboratory pioneered the effective use of kilns to dry wood by applying heat, a major improvement over the traditional air drying.

Wayne Anderson recalls working at the kiln when he was young. "We'd pile wet lumber on a car, 8 feet wide and 12 feet high, then roll the car in. The kiln was fired with wood shavings. When the wood was dry, we'd roll the car from the kiln to the planing mill. We only did this for wood that was sold at retail. That was the only stuff that had to be very dry." The rest was 'stickered'—had small sticks inserted between the layers of green lumber to improve air circulation—and allowed to air dry.

Hedstrom Lumber replaced horses in the 1940s with an International Harvester bulldozer.

The eight Hedstrom boys worked around the mill in various capacities, and as they came of age, all but Lawrence and Art joined Andrew Hedstrom & Sons as full-time workers. Daughter Lucille, who married A. B. "Otey" Walker, also stayed on for a career as company secretary and bookkeeper. Frances also was nearby, though she devoted her working years to teaching school. And Mildred had a home up on central Maple Hill, just a long stone's throw from Alma's home.

"Dad never asked us to stay here in the mill and community," Andy told Gareth Hiebert of the St. Paul Pioneer Press in 1964. "I don't think he ever mentioned it. We just stayed if we wanted to, and most of us did."

Each of the sons who stayed worked at one time or another at all of the jobs associated with running a logging and lumber company. All of them worked in the woods in the winter and in the mills in the summer. But over time, all of them also developed specialties.

Roy, for example, became the sawyer and was always the presumed "boss."

Phil bulldozing a skidway in 1945.

Herb operating a swinging trim saw.

Carl was a good mechanic, and in the early years was in charge of the logging camps. After he returned from service in World War II, he worked primarily keeping the equipment running and managing the company trucks. Carl suffered one of two serious injuries in the Hedstrom clan when a load of logs came off a truck at an angle and rolled over him, breaking both his legs.

Andy was the "engineer" of the family and the only one with any formal education—a year of college at Michigan Tech in Houghton, Mich., which was all the family could afford because of the Depression. Andy is described as having "a head for math" and being thoughtful. He was quite proficient at fabricating and

Breaking the Code

Growing up in the tip of northeastern Minnesota taught Arthur Hedstrom how to fix things.

"I always figured that if somebody could design and build it, I could take it apart and fix it," he said.

That resolve and skill enabled Hedstrom to rise from lowly enlisted man to first lieutenant during his World War II service, and to spend much of his later time in the war building a machine that enabled America to decode the messages of one of our allies—Russia.

Although Russia was officially our ally, it was becoming clear that the post-war world would be a struggle between Soviet communist ideology and Western democracy. Knowing what the Russians were communicating was critical.

Hedstrom was assigned to create a machine that would duplicate the actions of the Russian code machine. The code breakers discovered that the Russians used a standard five-letter code,

but the task was made more difficult by the fact that the Soviets would send three to five messages at a time.

It became an all-absorbing problem, and Hedstrom would work on the machine by day and lose sleep over it at night. "Sometimes I would wake up in the middle of the night, and I'd have the solution to what had been stopping me during the day. It was crystal clear. And then I'd wake up in the morning, and it wouldn't make any sense.

"That's when I started sleeping with a flashlight and a notepad. When I woke up, all I needed to do was jot down my thoughts. It worked."

It took many months, but Hedstrom came up with the machine the Army was looking for…. One of the things that made Hedstrom happiest was that the machine he built to replace the Russian code machine could fit on a kitchen table top. Some time later, the Americans captured one of the real Russian code machines, and it was much larger. Hedstrom had managed to build a better, or at least a more compact, mousetrap.

Herb, Andrew, Marion and Art say goodbye as the boys enter the military. Herb joined the Coast Guard and Art was in the Army Signal Corps.

Because of the importance of these projects, Hedstrom was kept in the Army until late 1946. He had to sign papers saying he would not disclose any of the work he had been doing. He had been offered a job on the White House staff at that point, but decided it was time to be a civilian again.

—Adapted from "He was always good with machines," by Al Zdon, Minnesota Legionnaire, November 2007.

Roy **(center)** is sawing with Carl **(right)** setting and riding the carriage. The onlookers are unidentified.

fixing machinery, and managed many of the millwright chores, as well as being in charge of the planing mill.

In 1936, when Andy was 21, he had the idea to harness the water power of the Devil Track River to generate electricity. So he sent away to the University of Minnesota requesting design plans for a hydroelectric plant run by a water wheel. Howard recalls the wheel as 10 or 12 feet high by 3 feet across. His dad "bought the generator and batteries from the courthouse when distributed electricity came to town," Howard said. " The batteries were in the grandparents' basement, and wires went to our house, the grandparents' house, Roy's and Carl's houses and the mill. I think it was 110-volt DC. They used the Cat to dig a trench along the bank to the curve in the Devil Track upstream and feed that water into the pond across from Chris Hegg's (formerly Wes and Thelma's) house. The pond was dug with the Cat as well. I believe it was a 3-hp generator. Of course, there were just lights that were electric at that time. I believe REA

came in 1946, so that plant ran until then. The wheel house was there in my youth. "

Herb is described as an easygoing guy who did many things but gradually specialized in sales. For years, he managed the retail outlet.

Phil was "the Cat man," an artist with large machines, which he loved, and was especially at home working in the woods, building road, skidding and loading logs. Phil suffered a serious head injury and lost an eye when the hook on a logging chain broke; the chain recoiled and hit him in the back of the head, cracking his skull "like an egg shell," Wayne recalled. Against great odds, he survived and returned to the equipment and woods he loved.

Wes, the youngest, did numerous jobs in his younger days but then settled in as manager of the planing mill. He also emerged as the company's third leader, after Andrew and then Roy.

Phil on the "Cat" using an arch-frame skidder to skid a load of birch.

In his 1964 Pioneer Press feature celebrating the Hedstrom mill's 50th anniversary, Gareth Hiebert wrote, "The idea of a Hedstrom community just happened. The family owned the property and the boys wanted to stay in the mill. So when they picked out their schoolmarm to court and marry (Lawrence, Roy, Andy and Phil all married teachers), each son blocked out a piece of ground and built his home. The houses that stand in Hedstromville represent the changing concepts of American architecture during the last half century...."

" 'But one thing never changed,' Alma told Hiebert. 'Every house was built of wood—and every stick was Hedstrom lumber.' "

Although there is some disagreement in today's Hedstrom family about this, it seems clear that the sons tended either toward Alma's calmness or Andrew's fiery quick-on, quick-off temper. Phil, Herb and Wes are described as being more like Alma, with Roy, Carl and Andy as more like Andrew.

The fiery outbursts were, Howard and several others said, almost always aimed at inanimate objects. Wayne says when Carl got mad—"it was hard not to laugh sometimes" – it was always at equipment, not people. Several family members recalled a particularly hilarious outburst from Carl: At his house on Devil Track, he had a recalcitrant outboard that just wouldn't start. Finally, exasperated, he drove 10 miles to the mill, retrieved a sledgehammer, drove home and smashed the offending outboard to bits.

On the business end, immediately following the 1929 fire, the Hedstrom crew moved logging and lumber operations into the western portion of the Maple Hill area and Rosebush, which was an old township west of Maple Hill and north of Highway 61. Fall River originally was called Rosebush Creek. The portable mill was set up near Meridian Road, not far from where Andrew and his father-in-law, Olaf, had homesteaded some 40 years earlier.

In the winter of 1933-34, the logging/sawmill operation moved to the Colville area in Township 62 North, 2 East, sections 29 and 30, roughly between Durfee and Kimball creeks. These were the two sections immediately northeast of the original logging site at the intersection of Lindskog Road and County Road 60. Operations remained there until 1939.

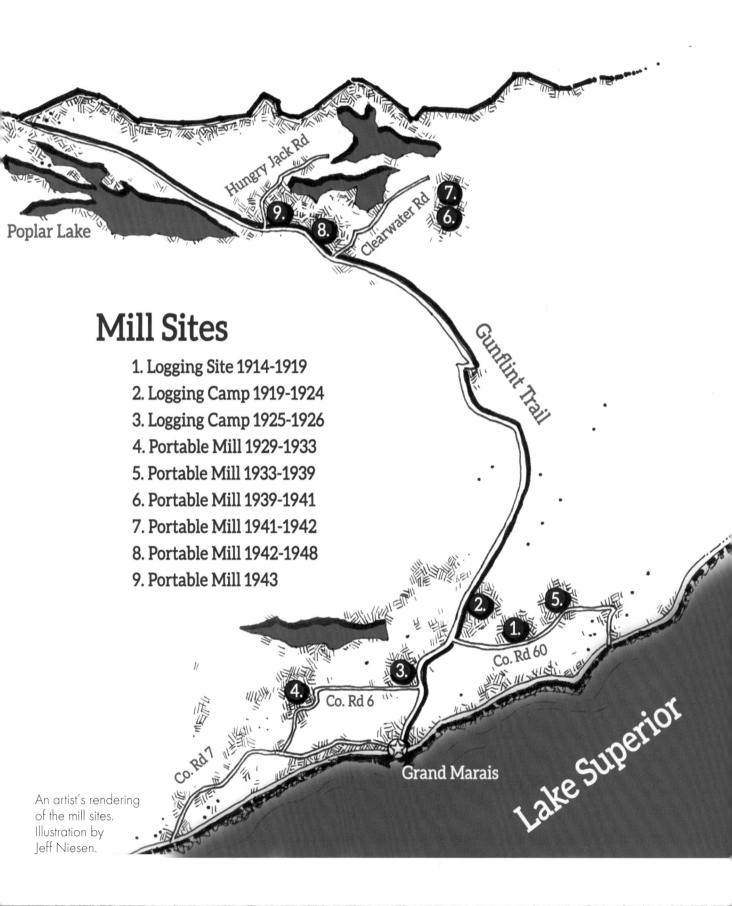

Mill Sites

1. Logging Site 1914-1919
2. Logging Camp 1919-1924
3. Logging Camp 1925-1926
4. Portable Mill 1929-1933
5. Portable Mill 1933-1939
6. Portable Mill 1939-1941
7. Portable Mill 1941-1942
8. Portable Mill 1942-1948
9. Portable Mill 1943

An artist's rendering
of the mill sites.
Illustration by
Jeff Niesen.

Roy, Herb, Wesley, Andrew and Andy standing in front of the retail lumber storage shed at the sawmill in 1949.

From Colvill, the Hedstrom crew made a significant geographic leap to harvest a state timber sale near Alder Lake, now inside the Boundary Waters Canoe Area Wilderness. The camp was established between the south Arm of East Bearskin Lake and Little Alder Lake, Township 64 North, 1 east, section 9. They remained there two seasons.

One wonders if the sudden shift in operations to northern Cook County—totally out of character with what had transpired to that point—was due in part to the 1938 change in leadership: Andrew, now 68, retired and handed the company reins to Roy, who would remain in charge until 1972.

With the departure years earlier of Lawrence, it just naturally was assumed that Roy would replace Andrew. Partly that was the tradition of elevating the oldest son. Given the era, a significant role for the daughters apparently wasn't seriously entertained, either by the parents or by the daughters themselves. By age, Frances, Mildred and Lucille all outranked Roy.

But Roy wasn't just the oldest son: He also was unquestionably the man in charge by sheer force of personality, which might best be described as somewhat "severe." Both Herb and Wayne said the younger second-generation Hedstrom brothers feared incurring Roy's wrath for misbehavior far more than they feared their parents.

Roy is described variously by the Hedstroms now alive as "a tyrant," "bossy," "the enforcer" and "all business when he was sawing logs but otherwise pretty mellow." Roy did not have children of his own, but the home that he and his wife, Sophia, kept near the mill was a frequent destination for Hedstrom grandchildren, and Sophia offered piano lessons to several.

That Roy's elevation to company head was such an accepted event within the family probably played a critical role in the company's survival. Especially in a family with 12 children, disagreements over generational succession can literally cause a company to disintegrate.

It's also quite obvious, given the record of what happened between 1938 and 1972, that Roy was exceptionally adept at guiding the company toward the family's vision of growth and prosperity. In 1946, the company formally incorporated as Andrew Hedstrom & Sons. Roy was president, Andy was vice president, Carl was treasurer and Wes was secretary.

Also in 1946, a man joined the company who was, by all accounts, a mechanical genius. Hilding Bjorklund (whom the youngsters called "Welding Beercan," Howard recalls) was by then in his 50s and a World War I veteran. Initially, Margaret wrote in her 1964 company history, they had Hilding piling lumber, but, "it was soon discovered that he was wasting his talents.... The Hedstroms feel that the mill would not be what it is today had it not been for Hilding's know-how and ingenuity. The machines he rebuilt or built 'from scratch' are too numerous to mention.... It is doubtful if there is a piece of equipment on which he has not worked...and the improvements are many that he has made on them."

Master mechanic Hilding Bjorklund working with a band saw grinder in 1960.

Everyone vigorously affirms Margaret's judgment. Of the hundreds of people Hedstrom Lumber Co. has employed over the years—the list of family names make a veritable "Who's Who" of Cook County —probably no one was as highly respected as Hilding Bjorklund.

"We've still got some of the equipment Hilding made," Howard said. "You pick up something of his and turn it over in your hand and wonder, 'How in the heck did he make that?' And he was fast. You think this precision work would be slow and methodical, but he just whipped it out."

Wayne, who joined the company later and became an outstanding filer, millwright and machinist in his own right, credits Hilding with teaching him an enormous amount. But Hilding wasn't always a willing teacher, Wayne said. "If he was in the mood, sometimes he'd answer your questions, but sometimes not. So I'd try to watch him work. But if he caught you, he'd wave you away. You could be on the opposite side from his light, and he'd say, 'Move, move, you're blocking my light.' So I got very good at watching him without him catching me at it."

From their camp near East Bearskin and Little Alder, the Hedstrom crew moved, in 1941, to the east half of the south quarter of section 10, Township 64 North, 1 west, near the junction of Clearwater Road and the Gunflint Trail. Only

one season passed there before the next move, to a new camp between the north arm of East Bearskin and a lake then named Sucker Lake, now Moon Lake. They worked there until 1944, although "they" were much diminished by World War II: Wes, Carl and Herb left to serve in the military. Phil and Andy were ineligible because of physical problems, and Roy was too old.

The next move was to a point on an old railroad grade south of Swanson's Lodge on Hungry Jack Lake. That camp lasted only one year before the crew moved back to the old site between East Bearskin and Sucker Lake, where they remained until 1947-48, when sawmill operations moved back to the home place in what the family calls "the homecoming." By then, trucks and heavy machinery were replacing horses both in the woods and for hauling logs and lumber. Plus, available timber was becoming too highly scattered to be efficiently serviced from central camps, even those that were moved every year or two.

Several of the old Hedstrom logging and sawing sites are still in evidence—sawdust doesn't decompose quickly, Howard says. Kent Anderson, grandson of Charles and greatgrandson of Andrew, made his way in the spring of 2013 to the Sucker (Moon) Lake camp and found both the inevitable pile of sawdust along with bits of old machinery.

PERMANENT MILL

With the 1948 "homecoming," as Margaret appropriately termed it, Andrew Hedstrom & Sons started on a process of change that would accelerate as the years passed. The portable, diesel-powered sawmill was brought home and installed in the mill so that all sawing and finishing now got done at the home place. Hedstrom crews still spent winters in the woods logging timber for the spring sawing and summer planing seasons. But the camps now were strictly logging operations, under Phil's direction.

The planing mill showing Andy planing at left with Bill Erickson at right.

Carl had run the camps until he left to join the service during the war; after he returned, he shifted his attention to mechanical maintenance and trucking, though he still put his hand in mill work when needed.

Horses, the mainstay of logging operations, rapidly were being replaced by trucks. Indeed, by the early 1950s, Phil Kruse—Andrew's grandson, son of Helen Hedstrom Kruse and Jerry Kruse—affectionately recalls, only two Hedstrom horses, Tom and Jerry, were left. They lived in the home place barn—playground for Phil and his cousins—and apparently were used for putting up hay and other farm chores.

By this time, all the Hedstrom children were fully grown and most were married. Lawrence had moved to Duluth and was pursuing a business career; Art was working for Bell Telephone, but all the other sons were fully engaged in the logging and lumber business.

Andrew was retired, of course, but he still kept a close eye on operations. In 1948, he made his first return visit to Sweden, more than half a century after his departure. He flew, and his account of the trip in the News-Herald makes clear it was quite an ordeal. He also did not tell anyone he was coming, but after a bit of confusion, he connected with his family and had a satisfying visit.

In this era, the Hedstrom mill was known for producing just about everything needed to build a house, including the windows. "It was customer driven," said Jack, "and the customer was Andrew. When he left the sawmill, he went back to building houses. And what he needed to do that, the mill produced." So in a real sense, Andrew propelled the Hedstrom focus on retailing.

The mill also maintained a close relationship with the Art Colony of Grand Marais, supplying the framing materials the artists required. "That was my father," Jack recalls. "He was a real craftsman. They had a moulder (the one Al Fenstad had acquired in Chicago in the '30s), and dad would make the knives for it and turn out all sorts of frames. We have a number of Mary Pratt paintings we got in

Carl and a 1946 International truck loaded with white pine from Stoney Creek, circa 1955

return for the frames dad made for her."

Bob Pratt, son of artist Mary Pratt and village dentist Dr. Harry Pratt, recalls that Andrew not only built homes, he rehabbed them: He purchased, moved and remodeled numerous homes in Grand Marais. Bob's parents were close friends with a number of Andrew and Alma's children and their spouses. Bob recalls that when he was about 6 or 7 years old, in the 1940s, Andrew was buying houses on the west side of Grand Marais, moving them to new lots and rehabilitating them. He hired Bob and a friend to straighten the old nails. "Nails were hard to come by," Bob said. "I got a dime a day."

Phil with a drag of logs.

Bob also recalled Phil doing landscaping around the rehabbed houses with a bulldozer. "He'd hold me on his lap while he worked and let me pull the levers," Bob said. The bulldozer enchanted the youngster, and he saw where Phil kept the key, under the seat. So when Phil wasn't around, Bob retrieved the key and started the dozer. Fortunately, his couldn't or didn't know how to run the pedals, and by the time he'd figured that out, Phil had caught on, and moved the key. But Bob did figure out that he could move the machine using the battery, and promptly ran it down.

Phil was Bob's favorite, a stand-in uncle, as several of the Hedstrom men were, after Bob's father died when he was 11. "I hated to see Wes and Phil and Herb get married," Bob said, "because it meant I wouldn't get to spend so much time with them. I hated to see them get that old."

Bob recalls when Phil suffered that horrible head injury in the woods, "I would sit by his bed for hours, hoping for him to get well."

Bob's warm recollections of the Hedstrom clan tell a lot about the kind of family they were. Of Alma he said, "I remember her kindness. She was very soft-spoken, just calming to be around. Andrew was kind, too, but he was kind of crisp."

"When I would stay with Andrew and Alma ... she knew I liked potatoes, so she would make sure I had potatoes for lunch and dinner. Sophie, Roy's wife, taught me to read, and Jane, Herb's wife, always sent me a birthday card when I was older, about the only card I would get. Lucille had polio when she was young and had a leg that was badly withered. She frequently would break it, but despite that, she kept the most glorious garden, just spectacular. And she made the best rye bread in the county. She'd call and tell me to

Andrew and Alma in front of their home, now owned by Burt Bockovich.

The Andy Hedstrom house in 1955. The house, later owned by Howard, burned in 2006. He rebuilt in the same location.

The Hedstrom family in 1948. **Seated in front, from left:** Andy, Hildur, Howard (baby), Frances, Jack (toddler), Jane and Herb. **First row standing:** Mildred, Tom, Diane, Phil Kruse, Ken Kruse, Lucille, Marshall Fenstad, Elizabeth Ann Hedstrom. **Second row standing:** Phil holding Stan, Wayne, Ruth, Charles, Art, Alma, Andrew, Helen, Mary Patricia Hedstrom, Elizabeth Fenstad, Wes, Carl, Jerry Kruse, Evelyn, Lawrence, Florence, Charles Anderson, Alfred Fenstad, Sophie and Roy.

The sawmill in 1957. Logs entered the mill on the left side. After trimming, lumber slid out on the right side on the green chain (the conveyor on which freshly sawn "green" lumber leaves the mill), then was graded and separated into piles.

come get a loaf. The entire family was just very nourishing, unconditionally positive to me."

Andrew also continued his lifelong passion for gardening after leaving the mill. In her booklet, "And the Lord God Watched Over Them," Frances recalled that Andrew had "built a hotbed on the south side of the workshop, where he raised seedlings for the vegetable and flower gardens. He laid out a beautiful formal flower garden with raised beds, fenced in to keep the livestock and chickens out. He acquired a piece of land half a mile east where there was better soil where he raised potatoes, rutabagas and lots of cabbage. In his retiring years, he had a garden back of the house with several varieties of vegetables and strawberries. Mamma helped with that, and had flowers in front of the house and a beautiful row of sweet peas out by the clothesline." Andrew was known for his beautiful, handmade wooden berry baskets, which he could turn out in a flash.

On the business side, in 1951, a new planing mill replaced the building that had been in service since 1929. That was followed in 1955 by construction of an entirely new sawmill on the north side of the Devil Track where the mill is located

Planing mill, warehouse and office in 1955.

today. The old portable sawmill, brought back to the home place in '48, was replaced by major upgrades: a new hydraulic log turner, an automatic carriage to move the logs back and forth for the initial saw cuts, new planers and matchers (a matcher trims board edges for such applications as tongue and groove). Two years later, in 1957, another major innovation was introduced when band saws were installed in the sawmill to replace the traditional circular saws.

Inside the sawmill looking out the green chain in the 1950s.

Andrew standing in front of the Ross forklift being driven by Andy with a lift of lumber from the mill.

In the 1950s, the Hedstroms moved their growing retail operation from the mill itself into a new building built for that purpose. As the business continued to grow, they found themselves again short of space. So in 1961, they purchased the Gipson Lumber Yard, on the site now occupied by Sawtooth Lumber on the western edge of Grand Marais, as their retail outlet and converted the old store at the mill into company offices. Herb, who had managed the retail side for years, became the general manager at the new retail outlet, assisted by his son, Alan, and Phil's son Stan, among others. Over the years, the retail outlet expanded several times and offered a comprehensive supply of lumber, hardware, paints and other building supplies.

At the same time, and at Wes' urging, the company was expanding its wholesale business. From a small fraction of sales in the 1950s, the wholesale operation gradually would supplant retail completely, until, in the 1990s, Hedstrom's became almost entirely a wholesale seller of wood products to just a handful of buyers scattered around the Midwest. This suited Herb just fine. In 2013, he recalled that he "really enjoyed" working with the wholesale buyers, whom he came to know well. Retail, he said, was messy and required dealing with too many people.

That old nemesis, fire, also reappeared. A report in the Cook County News-Herald in 1956, on the occasion of an open house at the new sawmill, included an offhand note that the dry kiln had burned twice and been rebuilt. Indeed, dry kiln fires, while not an everyday occurrence, happened frequently enough that the Hedstroms learned to take them in their stride.

Life also brought to the Hedstroms, as it does to all families, the inevitable sad endings. "On Saturday, May 23, 1959, after working in the garden to prepare for the spring planting," Frances wrote, "Papa stuck his spading fork in the ground and put his gloves in the handle—ready for his next trip out. That evening he had a severe stroke and was taken to the hospital, where he died at noon the next day."

Roy sawing a white pine log with a band saw in about 1960.

Carl working as the setter, who rides the carriage and takes instructions from the sawyer.

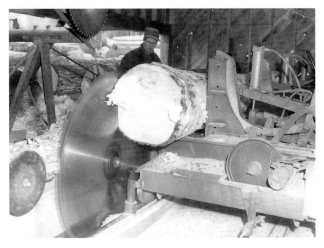

An earlier photo showing the circle saw, which was replaced by the band saw.

The new mill began operation in January 1956.

A New, Modern Mill

In January (of 1956), the (Hedstrom) company set in operation a brand new mill. It is a large building ... and it is located east of the old portion of the Gunflint Trail that swung around the Hedstrom home. Here a crew of about eight to 10 men are employed. Others are employed in the woods, on trucks, in the planing mill and machine shop.

About 16,000 feet of lumber is sawed daily.

The logs—pine and spruce mainly—are hauled on trucks from their stand southeast of Greenwood Lake, a haul of about 30 miles.

The logs are piled before an open door on the northwest corner. An operator rolls the logs against a huge claw, which, operated by air compression, tosses the big logs up on the carrier as if they were matches. The sawyer signals the setter (the man who rides the carriage) the set he wants. The sawyer moves a lever, and the carriage moves forward, pushing the log through the whirling circle saw. The log moans as it surrenders one board after another until it has all become either usable lumber or culled slab.

As each piece of lumber drops from the saw, it starts its ride up an endless belt, where another operater decides its width dimensions and guides it through a set of much smaller saws. Some slab by-passes and starts its ride out to the slab pile that is afire. The good lumber continues down another endless belt to the next operator, who sorts the good from the bad and end-cuts the good boards. These continue out a side opening of the building where two or three pilers are ready to grab them. They sort them as to size and pile them for delivery to the dry kiln. An elevator on a tractor lifts the pile and moves on to the kiln.

Down at the planing mill, skilled workers plane the boards and get them ready for market. Some of the lumber becomes window frames. In the hands of skilled operators it can become almost any standard wood building material.

The power is furnished by a diesel motor and electricity.

With so much machinery around, a machine shop is maintained at all times. Several home-made devices have been invented to cope with certain needs. Repairs are continually being made.

A $10,000 planer has just been installed to replace outmoded equipment in the planing mill.

When the lumber has been processed, it is trucked away, much of it sold outside the county to a ready market.

—Adapted from Cook County News-Herald, March 8, 1956.

Shown at the 50th anniversary from left: Roy, Andy, Wes, Phil, Carl and Herb.

Throughout most of the 1948-64 era, Roy wore three hats: He was president of the company, general manager of the operation and sawyer. But as production expanded, his management duties also grew. In 1962 he gave up his sawyer duties to focus on managing the operation. Roy also became more and more active in trade organizations and began moving up the ladder in the Timber Producers Association, headquartered in Duluth, culminating in his election as president in 1963.

That also was the year of two momentous changes for the Hedstrom company. First, it gave up its logging operations entirely and would now depend on timber cut by others. The Hedstroms would still bid on timber sales, as they do to this day, but henceforth they would contract out the actual harvesting. They would also purchase timber from independents who bought and cut timber on their own.

The second change followed naturally from the first: The company moved its sawmill and planer to year-round operations. It was the end of an era and of the seasonal rhythm: Cut timber in the winter, saw in the spring, plane in the summer and fall. Now Hedstrom was strictly a lumber operation—and a highly automated operation at that. First with Hilding Bjorklund, then with Wayne, Howard and Dean (Art's son), the Hedstrom mills constantly were trying some new device that might improve efficiencies, reduce labor or increase safety. For a mill on the edge of nowhere, it was a remarkable generator of new approaches to lumber milling.

Alma and Andrew at their 60th wedding anniversary in 1958.

EXPANDING BUSINESS

The Hedstrom clan took time out in 1964 to celebrate the 50th anniversary of their company founding but were soon back to work. Early in 1965, they continued their aggressive efforts to both mechanize their plant and wrest more products from every log they processed. Production already had grown exponentially: From the mill fire in 1929 to the 50th anniversary in 1964, the mill's output had grown 30-fold, from 100,000 board feet to 3 million board feet a year.

A load of finished lumber leaves the mill in the 1970s, driven by Roy Lindskog.

Wayne Anderson does maintenance on a band mill.

Earl Anderson grading lumber in 1965.

In 1965, both the march toward an ever-more mechanized plant and the equally strong effort to squeeze more from each log were served by the addition of a debarker, which stripped each log of its outer layers before it arrived at the carriage for the initial cuts by the head saw. This helped reduce the need to continually resharpen the head saws, which dulled quickly cutting through bark and the foreign material embedded in it.

The Hedstroms also took advantage of the debarker installation to make general improvements to the mill. Available voltage to run machinery was increased from 220 to 440; the walls were pushed out numerous feet on the south and west sides, the dirt floor was excavated to improve headroom for conveyors, conduits and other mechanical items, and a cement floor was poured.

Following quickly on the debarker was a chipper, which converted slab wood to chips sold to the paper mill in Thunder Bay, Ontario. Until installation of the debarker, the slabs retained the bark, which reduced their usefulness. And until the chipper was added, the slabs had simply been burned. Together, these two pieces of machinery made it possible for the Hedstroms to sell paper-quality chips. Sawdust and bark was about all that remained in the mill waste stream.

Wayne Anderson benching a band saw in 1965.

Lou Terizzi running the trimmer in 1970.

Left: Phil stands behind a device called a gang edger, which helped the mill produce lumber more efficiently.
Above: Howard Houglum edging.

The sawmill with the teepee burner and chip bin. Slabs were chipped and sent to a paper mill in Thunder Bay. Sawdust was burned.

An overview of the mill.

In 1968, the Hedstroms built a new, larger dry kiln and added a new gang edger—a saw that could cut multiple boards from one log simultaneously. Improvements to mill machinery also were made during a six-week fall shutdown in 1970. At the end of that shutdown, the mill set a record for lumber sawed in one day: 24,000 board feet. A Cook County News-Herald article that fall reported that the Hedstroms sent one truck daily to Thunder Bay with chips and two trucks daily with wholesale lumber to central Minnesota, Fargo and Moorhead. The Hedstroms also began to saw birch and aspen, in response to the development of new specialty markets, and that lumber went to Minneapolis.

The upgrades of 1970 were followed in 1971 by addition of a Cleereman carriage, a line-bar resaw and a merry-go-round (a device that returns once-sawn lumber for successive cuts until it is entirely reduced to the desired size). The Hedstroms estimated that these improvements alone would increase output by 30-40 percent. A year later, the dry kiln was expanded, and a new sawdust-burning boiler was installed to heat the entire mill, including the dry kiln. A new repair shop also was added in 1972.

Erecting the new sawmill building in 1982.

In 1976, the Hedstroms purchased two steel buildings from the site of the old veneer plant near Lake Superior a mile west of Grand Marais. The buildings were taken apart and reassembled at the mill. A smaller building was made into a machine shop, while the larger one was divided in two. One half was devoted to a new plant for resawing and surfacing aspen and birch. The other half was used as a covering for lumber sorting. For the first time ever, all of the mill work had moved into indoor quarters that could be heated in winter and where workers were protected from the elements in all seasons.

The Cook County News-Herald of Oct. 13, 1977, reported on the new buildings: "The larger building...has been outfitted with a variety of equipment that will increase the speed and efficiency of the entire mill operation.

"The building includes a new breakdown hoist, a board sorting device, a band resaw and a 30-inch double surfacer.

"The finishing touches are still being completed on the new facility, but portions of it are expected to start earning their keep sometime later this fall.

Sawyer Mike Kimball in 1970. Log setting was then done automatically, rather than with someone riding on the carriage.

A gathering of family members, **from left:** Lucille Hedstrom Walker, Charles Anderson, Gerry Kruse, Helen Hedstrom Kruse, Mildred Hedstrom Anderson, Linda Hedstrom Noble, Sophie Olson Hedstrom and Roy Hedstrom.

Alma **(front)** at the 50th anniversary with Herb, Sophie, Roy, Evelyn and Lucille.

Shown in March 1997, are Jack, Roy, Jonathan, Howard and Tom.

Longtime bookkeeper Thelma and husband Wes on one of their many trips.

"The facility will eliminate a lot of hand work presently being done at the mill. The automation will not mean a reduction in the number of employees, but is seen as a step to allow the mill to eventually grow more. Hedstroms currently employs over 50, counting those who work at the retail yard.

"The buildings and equipment represent an investment in the neighborhood of $140,000. Some of the equipment was purchased used on the West Coast.

"The new facility will be fascinating to watch. Large stacks of rough lumber, or packages, are carried over to the breakdown hoist. This device raises the wood, allowing the boards to slide, one layer at a time, onto a conveyor system.

"The operator, working at a control panel, can direct the boards three ways. They can be sent rough to a grading area, they can be directed to the surface, or they can be sent over to the resaw.

"The boards can then be directed via conveyor systems back to the grading area. Here they are sorted and moved to a large stacking mechanism that moves them out of the building. Many parts were engineered and custom built by Hedstrom employees over the past several months.

Alma Hedstrom.

Roy Hedstrom.

In front from left: Mark Anderson, Alice Bauer, Matt Anderson, Rolf Anderson, Bob Hedstrom and David Eckel. **Sitting:** Evelyn Hedstrom, Judith Olson, Philis Anderson, Ann Hedstrom. **Standing, front:** Helen Kruse, Ruthanne Hedstrom, Mildred Anderson and Frances Fenstad. **Standing, back:** Roy Hedstrom, Lucille Walker, Carol Eckel, Phyllis Bauer, Sophie Hedstrom, Hildur Hedstrom, Jeanne Hedstrom, Wayne Anderson, Charles Anderson, Ken Bauer, Thelma Hedstrom and Wes Hedstrom.

"While many employees provided ideas for the system, much of the designing was done by Howard Hedstrom and Wayne Anderson."

These also were years of human transition as well. Alma, who had lived to join in the 50th anniversary celebration, died two years later, in 1966, at age 87. Now the mill was entirely in the hands of the second and, increasingly, third generation of Hedstroms.

Roy retired completely in 1972, though he kept his hand in the politics of timber and lumber, and in 1973 was elected first vice president of the Northern Hardwood & Pine Manufacturers Association, headquartered in Green Bay, Wis.

Following his retirement, his brothers—except Andy, who retired early because of ill health – took turns as company president: Carl, 1972-78; Herb, 1978-83; Phil, 1983-86; Wes, 1986-90. Generally, their terms coincided with the years leading up to their retirement, and they were mostly honorary titles. True management of the company moved from Roy to Wes, the youngest. Although it wasn't a title used frequently among the Hedstroms, the best way to think of Wes' role from 1972-1986 was "general manager." He was clearly the guy in charge, although responsible to the board of directors. It appears to have been a stroke of genius for managing the transition: Not only was Wes capable, he also was Alma's son—calm, even, attentive to what others

Roy, Carl and Andy greet Senator Ray Higgins in 1964.

Rough lumber in the lumber yard.

thought, collaborative. Leadership succession is a critically important issue for any enterprise, but particularly for a family business. The Hedstroms handled it extremely well.

Hilding Bjorklund, the magician millwright, retired in 1969 and was replaced by his protégé, Wayne Anderson, who had joined the company in 1960. Eventually, third-generation workers also would include Jack, Howard and Tom, Andy's sons; Stan and Ed, Phil's sons, and Alan Hedstrom, Herb's son. Later, Steve Noble, husband of Linda and son-in-law of Wes and Thelma, would join as financial manager for the company, a position he held for about five years—doing critical work, as it turned out. Lucille, who had served as bookkeeper for decades, also retired in 1970. Her place was taken by Thelma, Wes' wife.

Also in the 1970s, the shavings baler was replaced by a shavings bin: A new vendor, Wood Shavings Co. of Pine River, Mn., wanted the shavings in garbage-sized plastic bags. So a bagging operation was established that, in the early-1980s, led to the "bag ladies," an intrepid group of women who bagged the shavings and loaded them into semitrailers. Karen Neal, a bag lady for 14 years, provides a colorful account of this work elsewhere in this volume.

The 1970s also were the years of the huge ruckus over congressional action to grant full wilderness protection to the Boundary Waters. The Hedstroms, who until that point had milled mainly large, first-growth white pine, mostly from the Boundary Waters area, were strong supporters of multiple use. But they were not very visible in the political fights that took shape over the wilderness designation. Instead, they confined their efforts and comments to the quiet, decorous channels of the timber associations to which they belonged.

"We were politically naïve," Jack said. "When they passed the Wilderness Act in 1964, they said, 'Don't worry; we'll still have multiple use and logging and motors and all that.' Then in 1978, they said, 'Ah, we were just kidding,' and they passed the Boundary Waters wilderness legislation." And logging in the BWCA came to a sudden and total stop. The 1978 legislation had a huge and immediate impact: From a mill specializing in large white pine, the Hedstroms quickly became a mill that sawed mostly smaller timber from a larger variety of species, including birch and aspen.

One of the first adaptations Hedstrom Lumber Co. made was installation of a short-log mill that required a small crew and could handle the 8-foot logs that were increasingly becoming available. Although that mill only lasted until late 1981, it allowed the mill to double its production despite the loss of the BWCA timber.

The 1981 mill fire.

"It's kind of idiotic that the Hedstrom mill exists at all," Jack said. "If you draw a 100-mile circle around the mill, you won't find a lot of harvestable timber. There's Lake Superior and Canada and the Grand Portage reservation and the Boundary Waters, and not a lot else."

Despite all the challenges, the 1970s were a prosperous decade for the Hedstrom clan. The mill had been significantly improved, output had increased dramatically, new product streams had been created from what had been mill waste, and the third generation of Hedstroms was being successfully integrated into mill operations. As the 1980s dawned, the future seemed secure.

That was an illusion: Their old enemy, fire, made a devastating surprise appearance on Dec. 1, 1981: The entire sawmill burned to the ground. Suddenly, it was 1929 all over again, time to start from scratch, just as Andrew had been forced to do a half-century before.

Aftermath of the 1981 fire.

EVERYTHING BUT THE SQUEAL

Just a year before the disastrous 1981 mill fire, the Hedstroms had brought aboard Steve Noble—husband of Linda Hedstrom Noble, Wes and Thelma's daughter—to serve as chief financial officer. It proved an extremely fortuitous hiring.

Steve set about relieving a number of financial pressures that were weighing on the company as it struggled to survive a seriously depressed lumber market. One of his first efforts was liquidating a logging operation the Hedstroms had purchased from Stan Pelto several years earlier.

An aerial view of the present mill.

From left: Wes, Howard, Wayne and Jack in 1989.

Buying Pelto out was a nostalgic throwback to the days when the Hedstroms were both a logging and a sawmill company, but it was problematic in several ways, Steve said. Most important, it was losing money. With the mill running at perhaps 30 percent of capacity because of the troubled national economy, the company simply could not sustain an operation that siphoned off precious revenue.

That came as bad news to Phil and his son Ed. A few years before the Pelto purchase, Ed said, he and his father had started logging for the company again under a Forest Service program that granted timber rights in return for building roads to federal specifications. Phil and Ed loved working in the woods and running machinery; whether cutting timber or building roads, they were in their element. Purchasing the Pelto operation was an expansion of the road-for-timber effort.

Besides, Ed said, the machinery they acquired in the Pelto purchase was in bad shape. He and his father put a great deal of time into rehabbing it and were about finished when word came that the company was pulling the plug. Ed was very sad to hear that.

But in addition to losing money, a company logging operation created friction with the independent loggers on which the Hedstrom mill depended for much of its timber. If the Hedstroms purchased a timber sale and then used its own loggers to harvest the wood, the independents were frozen out, and they did not like that. Nor did they appreciate the Hedstroms bidding against them for timber sales. Losing money and friends wasn't a winning strategy, Steve concluded, "So I liquidated that part of the operation."

An ancillary issue involving the purchase of the logging operation was that Hedstrom Lumber Co. acquired rights to a plot of timber in what would become the Boundary Waters Canoe Area. An access road had been built into the sale plot, but before the timber could be cut, the wilderness had come into existence, and BWCA timber was off limits. It took years of litigation before Hedstrom Lumber Co. was able to secure partial payment for the timber it owned but could not cut.

Another revenue drain that required stanching would cause Steve and all the Hedstroms a good deal of heartburn, for it involved family finances. As the six sons who had followed Andrew into the business grew older, the company wrote them large annuities to see them and their families comfortably through retirement. Unfortunately, Steve said, "The brothers had a somewhat inflated notion of the company's value."

By the time Steve came into the company, it was making substantial payments to Roy and Andy, who had retired, and to the family of Carl, who had died. But the outflow of cash was more than the struggling company could sustain. "It became obvious as the recession hit and the mill burned that the value of the company was nowhere near what was used in the formula to set up the annuities. So it fell to me to renegotiate all of them," Steve said. It was a sensitive, difficult task.

"They were all understanding," Steve said. "They all wanted the company to survive, and they all agreed to smaller payouts that the company could afford." That Steve was able to accomplish this without alienating anyone speaks volumes to his skill not only with numbers, but with family diplomacy.

But Steve's most critical contribution to the survival of Hedstrom Lumber Co.—indeed the single most important factor in surviving the 1981 fire—did not seem that earth-shaking or even important when he did it: In the fall of 1981, roughly 90 days before the mill burned, Steve took out the first ever business-interruption insurance policy for Hedstrom Lumber. This type of insurance provides that in the event some disaster makes it impossible for a company to operate, the insurer will make up the revenue lost until the business can get up and running again. So the affected company can pay its outstanding debts and its ongoing expenses. It can continue to pay its workers and can afford to focus on getting back in business rather than liquidating.

Together with the property insurance payout on the value of the destroyed buildings and machinery, the business-interruption insurance gave Hedstrom Lumber a chance to make a comeback. But it did not guarantee success. That required a great deal of hard work, creative thought and application of copious amounts of traditional Hedstrom ingenuity.

At the center of the effort were millwright Wayne and maintenance manager Howard. The parallels with 1914 are uncanny: A Hedstrom and an Anderson working together to build a functioning mill from the ashes of a fire.

Wayne was truly his father's son: He brought the same skill and creative genius to the job of rebuilding this burned out mill as his father, Charles, had brought to fashioning a working mill from the burned-out hulk Andrew purchased from Ed Toftey in 1913. In similar fashion, Howard inherited from his father, Andy, a sophisticated mechanical aptitude, enhanced by an engineering degree from Michigan Technological University in Houghton, the same school his father had attended briefly.

The insurance payout from the 1981 fire did not provide sufficient money for the Hedstroms to simply purchase new equipment to replace what they'd lost. So Wayne and Howard began scouring the country for decent used equipment they might refurbish. In typical Hedstrom fashion, however, they did not simply seek to recreate the old mill; they wanted to build a mill that was better, that looked to the future.

Wes captured that attitude when he was interviewed by the Cook County News-Herald following the fire. "We had one of the most efficient producing mills in the lake states," Wes told the interviewer. "We have to look ahead—to what we want to do, what do we want to change. We have to look at the available timber sources. We can't overbuild; we have to build to meet the timber supply."

In a sense, the poor shape of the lumber market proved a godsend. When the fire hit, the main sawmill had been shut down for several weeks, and the mill was running only its short-log mill, producing at just 30 percent of capacity. "The company has an adequate inventory for 60 days," Wes told the News-Herald. "The building business is in the biggest depression since World War II, so if it turned around in January, we would be hurt. But since the markets are so poor, it wouldn't affect us as much if business was normal. We hope to maintain our old customers and whatever the market demands. We'll run two shifts if we need to."

By running two shifts, Wes was referring to the company's first order of business: setting up a portable sawmill as a temporary replacement. The fire also left a relatively new green chain building with little damage, so the temporary mill could be tied into that. A green chain collects boards as they come off the saws and moves them to an area where they can be sorted and stacked.

A portable mill was acquired in Wisconsin and installed in a small addition to the green chain building. Duane Ege

The new head saw in the mill not long after it was installed.

went to work restoring an edger from the small-log mill. And the chipper had survived the fire. The Hedstroms also had a stroke of luck in acquiring a large stock of lumber from a Canadian plant that lacked an edger. "It was beautiful black spruce," Howard recalled. "And we got it for less than the cost of timber," Wayne added. "All we had to do was finish it and sell it."

By running two shifts on the temporary sawmill, the company was able to keep almost the entire crew working. Layoffs were minimal.

An immediate concern was rebuilding the system that collected sawdust, chips and other waste from the temporary sawmill and moved it to the boiler. Not only was this necessary so the temporary sawmill could run, but the boiler was the only source of heat, and it was December. "We really had to hurry with that," Wayne said.

The fire also did not affect the planing mill, which still was located on the site of the original mill, south of the Devil Track River.

Even as all this work went on to get the temporary sawmill running, planning proceeded on building a new mill. The board of directors overseeing this work included Herb, Phil, Wes, Stan, Jack, Howard and Ed Hedstrom, Steve and Wayne. An immediate effort was made to preserve anything from the old mill that was remotely usable. "I cut off everything we could salvage," Wayne said.

Work also began as quickly as possible to clear away the rubble before cold weather froze the ground. Where they knew they would need to dig early in the spring, waste wood was dumped in an effort to keep the ground from freezing deep.

"We had lots of discussions on what the configuration

Wayne Anderson and Harry Lamson working on the new mill.

of the new building would be," Howard said, "what systems we would use, how we would place them and tie them together, the layout and design. And as we thought about where to place the new building, we had to work around the temporary sawmill, so it could keep running. There was a lot of engineering work to do."

It was decided the new mill building would be 80 x 200, shoehorned into an area previously home to the burned 60 x 105 foot mill. While negotiations started with Fred Anderson, a local contractor who would do the concrete work and erect the building, the Hedstrom team went shopping for machinery. Their list included: debarker, head rig, stop & loader, log turner, carriage, hydraulic shotgun carriage feed, edger, trimmer, twin resaw.

Of those pieces, the only two purchased new were the edger and the carriage feed. They did look at quite a lot of new machinery and visited a number of mills, but much of

what they saw they could not afford. Still, it gave them ideas about how they should equip their new mill.

"One salesman was describing all the things this piece of machinery he was selling could do," Wayne recalled. "Then he stopped and said, 'Oh hell, why am I telling you all of this? You'll just go home and build your own.' "

And they did build a great deal of their own. All of the equipment for transferring lumber from one machine to another, and all of the conveyor systems, were manufactured in house. Plus, Howard, Wayne and their crew spent a great deal of time refurbishing the used equipment they secured. "Most equipment like that will run for 20-25 years," Wayne said. "The stuff we rebuilt in 1982 and 1983 is still running" more than 30 years later.

Finding the used machinery was an adventure. At one point, Howard estimated teams from the mill had visited

Erland Shold loads a truck with chips bound for the paper mill in Thunder Bay.

12 states and three Canadian provinces in search of what they needed. For the equipment they would fabricate, the Hedstroms secured tons of iron stock for 10 cents a pound from an out-of-business contractor in Thunder Bay. They also bought a "pickup load" of tools from the same place, Howard said, items like grinders and drills.

The head rig they bought from an closed mill in Bagley, Howard and Wayne recalled. The carriage came from New York state. "We should have bought a new carriage," Wayne said. "But this place had two used ones, so we bought them and made one working carriage out of the two."

A twin resaw came from Tupper Lake, N.Y., the trimmer from Powell Lake, B.C. Wayne and Howard think perhaps the debarker came from Tupper Lake as well.

Once they got the used machinery home, work started in earnest on restoring and improving it. Many machines had old electrical controls, and the Hedstroms wanted to

upgrade all of that, wherever possible, to use computers to control the processes. Once the machinery was installed in the new building, Dean, Art's son, handled that. He explains:

"Before the 1981 fire the plant was all controlled manually; push buttons, foot switches, limit switches, levers and chains. There was some automation on the carriage, but not much. At the time my consulting engineering business was four or five years old. We specialized in assembly automation, industrial controls, communications and networking. Since Hedstrom Engineering was ticking along fine in St. Paul, I was able to personally spend a lot of time working on the mill controls and wiring.

"Howard and I sat back to back in what now is the maintenance office. Drawings flew off our desks. We had the rare opportunity for a clean sheet design. The prior plant had walls of manual and magnetic combination starters for motor controls. The new design utilized modular motor control centers. For controls we chose a specialized type

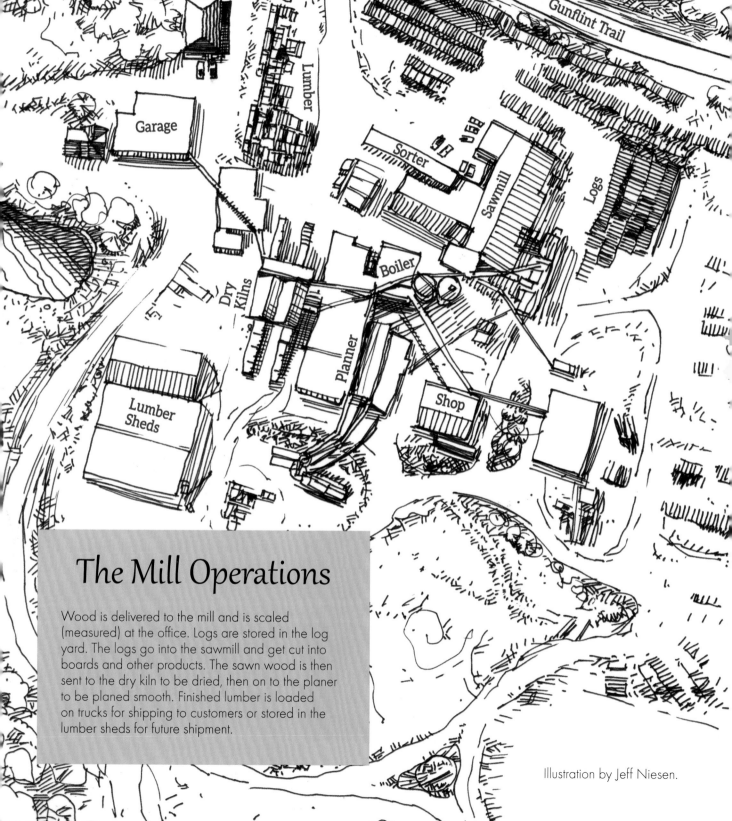

Office

Lumber

Garage

Gunflint Trail

Sorter

Sawmill

Logs

Boiler

Dry Kilns

Planner

Shop

Lumber Sheds

The Mill Operations

Wood is delivered to the mill and is scaled (measured) at the office. Logs are stored in the log yard. The logs go into the sawmill and get cut into boards and other products. The sawn wood is then sent to the dry kiln to be dried, then on to the planer to be planed smooth. Finished lumber is loaded on trucks for shipping to customers or stored in the lumber sheds for future shipment.

Illustration by Jeff Niesen.

The gang saw in the new mill makes up to 12 boards from one log.

of industrial computer called a programmable logic controller, PLC. This equipment is optimized for the industrial environment...."

Howard recalls many impromptu conferences involving Dean, Wayne, himself and pieces of soapstone. "Every engineer has a piece of soapstone in their pocket," Howard said. "We'd get talking, and soon we'd be down on the floor, drawing out ideas with soapstone.

Dean continued: "In addition to my professional registration I am also a licensed master electrician. This credential allows me to be to the Master of Record for the mill, thus avoiding the necessity of retaining a licensed contractor for our electrical construction and maintenance. During construction I 'supervised' two or three journeymen or apprentices. I do not recall any big problems with the startup. The log haul did not function as well as anticipated due to inconsistent slippage on the chains. Our efforts and success were noticed by A-B management; Howard and I were invited to make a presentation at an industry conference at their Milwaukee headquarters.

"Subsequent projects continued our choice of A-B for controls and automation. In the mid-'90s we retrofitted and upgraded the saw mill PLCs. By this time the equipment and ... the development software had advanced considerably.... We started the cutover Friday after shutdown and continued Saturday. On Sunday we tested subsystems as best as possible. On Monday morning I stationed one engineer at the end of a hall to take in trouble reports on a prepared form. These he passed to another engineer to triage the reports and outline a solution. Then the task was passed to a programmer for implementation or changes. This is a delicate operation as the plant is in operation and one needs to be extremely cautious not to introduce other trouble. In the end we had one trouble report, a timer function was off by an order of magnitude. This is a testament to the care and skill of the programmers.

"Another major project is the planer mill tray sorter. We designed a MS-Excel based configuration program for the operator interface. Compared with current implementations it is rather clunky (technical term), but thankfully still functioning with all the warts and scars.

"I have always tried to empower my clients with the resources and training to be self supporting. I do not need calls in the middle of the night for a problem that can be solved locally. Brian (Smith), Lenny (Bloomquist) and others have been able to keep up the maintenance, upgrades, and changes with occasional consultations."

But before any of that work could be done, the new mill had to be constructed. As soon as spring came in 1982, Phil was on his Cat preparing the ground for the new mill building. To fit it in required that all of the mill bins, three large ones, be moved. That proved to be a massive, difficult undertaking that involved a large crane barely capable of the job. But they got it done, all in one day, without incident.

By late summer 1982, the new mill building was well under construction, and the new machinery began to arrive. Getting it rebuilt, making the improvements they wanted, installing it in the new building and then crafting the connecting conveyors and transfers occupied the Hedstrom crew through the winter and into the spring of 1983. Most of it went into operation on Friday, May 13, 1983, although the twin resaw took several additional months to become operational. With the resaw running, the target set for the new mill was 45,000 board feet of finished lumber for each work shift. In two weeks, the new mill was capable of producing as much lumber as the 1914 mill had produced in an entire season.

While Dean ensured the mill remained up to date, keeping it running well fell to the filers, the millwright and other maintenance professionals. A sawmill is a noisy, dusty, violent place that puts enormous stress on machinery. But it needs to be a violent place that runs with excruciating precision. Dull, warped, stretched or cracked saws, worn bearings, slipping chains—these sorts of problems mean poorly sawn lumber, reduced production and, worst of all, down time when the expense clock keeps running but the revenue clock stops.

Asked to name the most important person in a sawmill, Howard and Wayne answered in unison: "The filer."

Howard explained: "Without the filer, you don't have a saw, and without a saw, you don't have a sawmill."

The filer's job is to ensure the saws perform flawlessly. That's not simple, and it takes years and years of experience to become a proficient filer. When it's operating, a band saw blade endures thousands of pounds of force and extreme heat, which can cause it to stretch, deform, crack and fatigue. To service a saw blade requires not just sharpening the teeth, but repairing cracks, correcting deformities, and leveling and tensioning the blade so it cuts flat and straight, and the mill gets lumber in the right dimensions.

The millwright is charged with keeping the entire mill finely tuned. Wayne Anderson, who served as both a millwright and a filer, explained that a good millwright is constantly looking for problems that are developing—a worn bearing, a weakening conveyor chain or belt, a crack in the metal infrastructure. When a problem is detected, the millwright sets about preparing a replacement part that is ready to go before it's needed.

Wayne and Howard said they both can go into a sawmill and tell by the sound whether it is running as it should. Developing an acute sense of what a properly operating mill sounds like is just one of the many skills a good millwright requires. Wayne served as millwright until his retirement in 1995. In 2001, his son Matt joined Hedstrom Lumber Co. and now has followed both his father and grandfather as the Hedstrom millwright. Wayne allows as how Matt is almost as good as he was. All still defer to Hilding Bjorklund as the master.

With a new mill full of Dean's latest controls and chock-a-block with machinery Howard and Wayne Anderson had found, refurbished and fine tuned, Hedstrom Lumber Co. in 1983 was ready to cut serious wood.

And it did, so much so that by 1984, it wanted to expand. But its bank accounts still had not recovered from the effects of the fire, so the Hedstroms sought state and county help to accomplish the expansion. With Steve leading the way, the Hedstroms applied for a $250,000 loan from the state under a new business loan program to which the Minnesota Legislature had just appropriated $6 million. The program was so new the final rules had not been written, and until Steve brought it to their attention, no one in the county was aware of it. The program required that the county apply for the loan, then, in turn, loan it to Hedstrom

Specialty products made by Hedstrom Lumber include siding, paneling and squares.

Lumber Co. When the company repaid the money, the county was allowed to keep the first $100,000 it collected, which it could then use to create a revolving loan fund for business.

With the loan money and a matching amount from Grand Marais State Bank, Hedstrom Lumber Co. proposed to increase mill production and introduce a new line of products it would market to the furniture and cabinet industries. The company estimated the expansion would add 12 to 15 jobs to the Hedstrom payroll.

Competition for the available $6 million inevitably would be fierce once word got out, so Steve urged the county board to act quickly. It did, approving the loan application with the understanding that the Arrowhead Regional Development Commission would prepare the application for a fee of $3,000. The loan was granted, Hedstrom Lumber Co. expanded its operations and the county revolving loan fund was created. To this day, the revolving loan fund is a

mainstay in Cook County's efforts to aid local businesses and create jobs.

At about this time in the mid-1980s, Wes Hedstrom began to look increasingly at how to smooth transfer of the family business to the next generation. He shifted more and more sales responsibility to Jack. Stan took on more and more oversight of mill operations. Howard got responsibility for external relations and political affairs. Alan, Herb's son, took on management of the retail store, and Ed, when he wasn't in the woods with Phil, managed the yard.

Despite the loss of BWCA timber, the 1981 fire and severe financial challenges, the Hedstrom Lumber Co. ended the 1980s in surprisingly good shape. They had a flexible, efficient, up-to-date mill sized right for the available timber, that used virtually every bit of every log and could turn on a dime to produce whatever the market demanded. Along the way, various improvements were made. In 1987, they established a small-log mill that was more efficient in handling—

The retail lumber yard in Grand Marais.

and getting the most boards from—the smaller-diameter pine logs that were available post-BWCA.

Adding the small-log mill again doubled their production, so that by 1989, on their 75th anniversary, output had reached 16 million board feet. In the brochure produced to celebrate that anniversary, the company noted its steady production gains, from less than 1 million board feet in 1950 to 16 million in 1989. And, it said, because of the small-log mill "we are now able to handle higher percentages of the available raw materials than ever before."

The mix of timber noted in the 1989 anniversary brochure is telling: From a company that, pre-BWCA, sawed white pine almost exclusively, it had evolved to the point that white pine made up only 26 percent; red pine, 22 percent; aspen, 22 percent; spruce, 18 percent; birch, 8 percent and jack pine, 4 percent.

Hedstrom Lumber Co. was Cook County's largest employer, with an annual payroll of about $1.7 million, and providing, as their anniversary brochure said, "stable, year-round income for 10 percent of the county's families, plus indirect earnings for another 8 percent. Despite the move to automation, our payroll continues to increase each year."

Not everything was rosy, of course. Fire put in another appearance in 1989 when the dry kiln burned, again, and

was rebuilt, again, but rebuilt better than before, of course.

When the Hedstroms stopped to celebrate 75 years in the wood-products industry, they had much to be thankful for and more to be proud of. The second and third generation of Hedstroms had well burnished Andrew's legacy. From the ruins of the 1981 fire had arisen an improved, forward-focused, solvent Hedstrom Lumber Co. as the last decade of the 20th century opened.

Alan Hedstrom managed the retail lumber yard.

The Bag Ladies

OF HEDSTROM LUMBER CO.

"Does your mom work?"

"Yes, she's a substitute teacher and a bag lady."

[Gasp!] "A what?"

"A bag lady. You know, she bags wood shavings up at Hedstrom's mill."

Four other Grand Marais women and I proudly claimed this title. We shared a job that can hardly be described as glamorous. In fact, some might call it horrendous! But for some strange reason, we "almost" enjoyed the job and found it raised our self-esteem a few notches.

For many years from the 1970s to the 1990s, the Wood Shavings Co. of Pine River, Minn., bought truckloads of wood shavings from Hedstrom Lumber Co. and other sawmills. They in turn sold them mostly to turkey farmers, who used the shavings as litter. Some truckloads were bulk loads of loose shavings. The majority, though, were bagged shavings—easier to handle, store and disperse. The garbage-can-sized bags were filled, tied and loaded on semitrailer trucks by people, not machines. I was one of those people.

When the shavings company needed a replacement bagger, the husbands of two friends suggested they split the job, and they jumped at the idea. It was strenuous and dirty, but it paid well, and it was part-time. They asked if I was interested, too; there was more work than they wanted. With dollar signs in my eyes and the "part-time" ringing in my ears, I quickly agreed, without ever seeing the bagging shed or watching the process involved.

Convincing the shavings company that three women could handle the job—previously done by a man—was more difficult. Finally, they agreed to a trial period. I'm sure they worried whether women were strong enough to do the work and willing to take the dirty job for more than two months.

We started work in October 1982. The three of us became five as the shavings output reached record proportions. We felt enormously overqualified in education (one of us was a music teacher, one an English teacher, two were art teachers, and one was a natural resources technologist) and under qualified in muscles and stamina. Never in my craziest imaginings did I

The Bag Ladies. **Front:** Deb White and Chris Conlan. **Back:** Karen Neal and Arlene Johnson.

think I'd ever work at a job like this. And stranger yet, I loved it.

The shavings were blown from the planing mill into a giant bin, under which we did our bagging. A chute at the bottom of the bin released the shavings into our ready bags.

We stretched the top edge of the bags around a steel hoop, opened the door at the bottom of the chute and filled each bag. An electrical foot pedal activated an auger in the bin to stir the shavings and ensure a free flow.

The actual work sounds elementary: Stretch a bag around the hoop, open the door, step on the foot pedal, kick the bag to pack it, tie the bag, put it on a trolley and, when four bags accumulated, load them on the semitrailer. The name of the game was efficiency, as we were paid by the bag, not the hour.

In reality, it frequently was more challenging and difficult. For one thing, the work was always terribly dusty. My "uniform" included a scarf over my hair, a mask that filtered the dust over my nose and mouth, goggles or glasses that had been defogged and a visor to provide a shelf above my face and catch dust. It wasn't a pretty picture. The rest of my outfit depended on the season. The building wasn't heated or air-conditioned. Whatever we wore, though, was usually old, tattered, faded and—after half an hour—very dusty.

Each of us had a different system to increase our efficiency. We eagerly shared tricks and tips that seemed to speed the work or make it easier. Because I found it difficult to load the truck with the respirator on (couldn't get enough air), I filled and tied 52 bags at a time, then loaded them. This gave me a break from the mask every hour, and allowed me to blow my nose and take a drink (luxuries!).

The variable that slowed us the most (other than cold weather) was the consistency of the shavings. Perfect shavings flowed quickly into the bag, settled well and weighed about 20-25 pounds. Extra-light shavings were lovely to load but very hard to pack—you kicked, shoved and shook the bags about three times longer than normal. Heavy shavings filled and packed well but were a real burden to load. The bags were laid down in rows and piled eight high. Hoisting a 60-pound bag beyond the fifth row was tricky: We started the next row, to create a step up. When we started, we all did about 30 bags an hour. After a couple of years, I was up to 45-55 bags an hour, depending on the variables.

Bagging in the heat of summer and cold of winter cut efficiency. In the summer, when the temperature was regularly in the 80s and above, our work clothes shrank and shrank, and our water breaks grew and grew. I wore short, baggy shorts, the thinnest sleeveless shirt, no socks but, of course, all my head gear. We teased each other that we were developing "bag lady syndrome:" shrunken faces under the mask because of all the sweating we did in the mask. This was not a glamorous job. In a five-hour shift, I would drink more than a gallon of water and never use the bathroom. My pores were constantly cleansed, from the inside out. Many times, we'd take a break and walk to the Devil Track River to dunk our heads and sit in the river, clothes and all.

The thing that hampered winter bagging the most is what cold does to plastic bags: They break easily. We had a heat lamp rigged up to warm the edges of the bags so they'd stretch over the hoop. But when it was 30 below, the bag cooled off in the two seconds between the heat lamp and the rim. Our bulky outfits and boots also slowed winter bagging. You just don't move as quickly with five layers on the top, three on the bottom and Sorels. Tying twine with gloves is not as automatic as bare hands. Breaks aren't needed as often for water, but there were certain hand-warming techniques that took time. But no matter what the air temperature, after filling, tying and loading my first 52 bags, I was toasty warm, even when the temperature in the shed was minus15, as it often was. The work was simply that strenuous. One bag lady had the misfortune of bagging 100 "mistake" bags: Ash shavings, which resemble graham flour, shouldn't have been blown into the bin. When bagged, they weighed about 100 pounds a bag. It was minus15 that day, but the woman said another 10 degrees colder would have been more comfortable.

Occasionally we had to shovel and poke around in the bin if the shavings weren't flowing properly. So it was up the ladder 20 rungs and into the wooden funnel, about 24 feet across and 30 feet deep. There were cross beams to walk on and boards along the sides to hold onto, but it wasn't built for people. The shoveling and poking was difficult because you constantly had to watch your balance and footing. Falling into the funnel was a constant and serious danger. It was scary, and we were very careful.

Being a bag lady was dirty, strenuous, dangerous and very uncomfortable in the winter cold. But I focused on the pluses. The sign on our door read: "Bag Ladies Health Spa." When I was bagging three days a week, I could eat anything and not gain a pound. In the summer heat, I ate like a pig and lost five pounds. I'd never had such good upper body strength—I could do pushups for the first time in my life.

The challenge of doing piece work was ongoing. Many people say they work harder for themselves than for a boss, and we bag ladies certainly worked for ourselves. The pay was good and worth the effort. The work was part-time and flexible. We shared, traded and substituted shifts. The camaraderie of the bag ladies was special. We usually worked alone, but such a unique common experience really bound us together. We all felt quite proud of the job we did. Perhaps our pride came from successfully taking over a "male" job, and we were so successful that the shavings company began hiring women at some of its other locations. That certainly made us smile.

When I went to work, I listened to lovely music on MPR, got a good physical workout and got paid a good wage. I learned to ignore the dust. I sometimes thought It would sound nice to say my field was "wood by-products" and that I was "second in command of packaging and distribution." But I've never been one to put on airs. "Bag lady" suited me just fine.

— *Karen Neal*

CHANGING WITH THE TIMES

As the 1990s came in, the second generation of the Hedstrom clan left the Hedstrom Lumber Co. stage. Roy, Herb and Phil had retired; Carl and Andy had died. Only Wes was left, and in 1990, he too retired. In 1984, Wes had won a seat on the Cook County Board, where he became a highly esteemed leader, playing much the same role as he had played at the mill. At age 66, he left Hedstrom Lumber Co. and devoted even more time to county business. He continued on the county board through four terms, until he gave up his seat in 2000.

The interior of the new mill. The log deck in center feeds the scrag saw at right. The debarker is in the background.

The small log deck is to the left and the large log deck is to the right.

Now the third generation took over. Operationally, Howard took on procurement (securing the timber) and maintenance, with Wayne at his side as millwright until he retired in 1995. Jack continued and expanded his sales and marketing portfolio, perhaps the most critical job in ensuring the company's continuing survival. Jack's go-to man in ensuring his work bore effective fruit was Merlyn Kiel, who had joined the company in 1984 and was sawmill foreman.

Their cousin, Ed Hedstrom, who had been with the company since 1970, was in charge of yard operations.

Jack and Howard divided up the world of external relations, with Howard taking on the political realm and Jack getting involved in the more technical associations. It was an inspired division of duties: Howard is a natural politician who takes maximum advantage of his physical stature, deep voice and open face to immediately cause you to want to hear what he has to say. Jack is the affable numbers nerd with a dazzling encyclopedic knowledge of the complexities of the American lumber grading system.

Howard became very active in Minnesota Forest Industries (MFI), a small policy and education organization of forest-product companies. It is the sister organization of Minnesota Timber Producers Association (TPA). Howard served long stints on the MFI board and twice served as its president. Meanwhile, Ed, who loved the logging and timber end of the business, served on the TPA board.

Howard also became active in the Lake States Federal Timber Purchasers organization, comprising federal timber purchasers in Minnesota, Wisconsin and Michigan. This group's role was to ensure its members' interests were heard and heeded as Congress and the U.S. Forest Service set policies and practices affecting the sale of timber on national forests. Howard chaired the organization for many years, a role that took him frequently to Washington, D.C., and into the corridors of power at the U.S. Department of Agriculture and the U.S. Congress, especially the House of Representatives.

Mutual frustrations with management of the nation's timberlands led Howard and a few other timber purchasers to form the Federal Forest Resource Coalition in 2010. Howard was chosen the inaugural president of the group, which quickly found it had touched a nerve, and not only among timber purchasers. The group grew rapidly to 650 members, including conservation groups and local governments in 28 states, with a combined payroll of $19 billion and almost 700,000 people.

"The wood products industry depends on healthy forests for our livelihood," Howard was quoted on the opening of the coalition's Washington office. "For too long, we've watched the forest service and other federal lands adopt a passive approach to management which threatens our mills and the health of their forests."

Jack, meanwhile, became active in organizations responsible for ensuring the integrity of the lumber grading certification process. Jack explains: "The certification has three levels of oversight. The mills have certified graders, regional associations—the Northern Softwood Lumber Bureau (NSLB) in our case—has inspectors who check the graders (12 times per year), and people who work for the American Lumber Standards Committee (ALSC) check the [NSLB] inspectors."

Jack became vice president of the NSLB in 1996 and president in 2002. The NSLB has one seat on the ALSC board, whose members are appointed by the U.S. Secretary of Commerce for five-year terms. Jack was appointed to the ALSC board in 1996 and is now in his fourth term. He also has been a board member of the Northeastern Lumber Manufacturers Association since 1997.

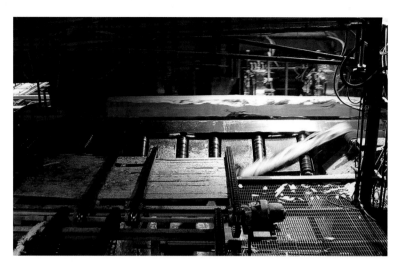

A slab coming off the carriage, heading for the chipper.

Twin resaw, which saws boards from slabs and also cants from the head saw.

Rob Revier working on a band saw in the file room.

The gang saw being sharpened.

One of the first new ventures for this third generation involved paper-quality chip production. For years, the Hedstroms produced chips from the small machine that crunched up their debarked slabs—the rounded outer bits of a log produced when the head saw makes its first cut. In 1991, the Hedstroms went full-bore into the chipping business: They installed a full-log chipper and secured a contract to provide chips to the Thunder Bay paper mill. This was a boon because every timber sale in this region produces a mix of sawmill timber and pulpwood. The new chipper allowed the Hedstroms to add value to the pulpwood instead of just selling the unprocessed logs to others. This new venture carried some risk because there are few industries more volatile than paper production. Unfortunately, the new chipping operation did not survive. In 1997, the Hedstroms lost their chip contract and were forced to shutter that portion of their Grand Marais operation.

Although the company had used flexibility and adaptation about as effectively as a company can in responding to the loss of its BWCA white pine, things were about to get a whole lot tougher. With the election of President Bill Clinton in 1992, the environmental community gained unprecedented access to power in Washington, and they were not inclined to look favorably on cutting timber on the U.S. national forests. Timber production plummeted nationwide: On the Superior National Forest, most important to the Hedstroms, it fell from historically high levels of more than 90 million board feet annually in the early 1990s until, in 2008, it stood at about one-third of that.

Fortunately for the Hedstroms, more timber was coming available from state and private lands. When Minnesota environmentalists worried about the impact of timber production, especially increased production for pulp and paper, sought an environmental impact statement, the state of Minnesota did something unprecedented: It undertook an assessment of all timberland in the state (private, national for-

A stock of sharpened band saws. It takes a lot of back-up saws to keep things running.

est, state forest) and an analysis of what level of harvest that timberland could sustain. The resulting Generic Environmental Impact Statement, released in 1993, found that the state's forests were in excellent shape and could sustain an annual harvest of 5.5 million cords annually.

So even if the national forests continued to de-emphasize logging, the loss could be made up from increased production from state and private lands.

Even then, however, there were large bumps in the road. When the Minnesota DNR offered a tract of old-growth white pine near Ely, known as the Kawishiwi Pines, for sale, Hedstrom Lumber Co. won the bidding. But before the logging could begin, explorer and musher Paul Schurke of Ely organized an effective protest. So effective, it was later discovered, that someone spiked many of the trees with nails. If the trees had been harvested and run through a sawmill, the effect on the saws, and potentially on the saw operators, could have been devastating. Ironically, spiking

trees doesn't save them: State policy is to identify which trees have been spiked and then cut them.

To avoid a potentially explosive showdown, Hedstrom's and the DNR negotiated a compromise with the protestors: The Kawishiwi Pines would be thinned but not clear cut, and Hedstrom Lumber also would receive timber from other state land nearby. The Kawishiwi Pines later were preserved as a state scientific and natural area. In a report on the eventual results of the thinning, the DNR reported, "During the 1991-1992 winter, 650,000 board feet of pine and over 400 cords of pulpwood species were harvested from 148 acres in this sale."

It is worth noting that thinning rather than clear cutting accounts for the bulk of the timber that comes to the Hedstrom mill today. The political and cultural environment within which sawmills must operate has changed dramatically over the last 50 years. That's why Wes Hedstrom took pains to note, in his introductory essay to the 75th anniver-

Large logs heading for the head rig.

sary brochure, "As one of Minnesota's leading sawmills, we are acutely aware of the need to balance production with the principles of good forest management and conservation." It's also why Hedstrom Lumber Co. has, for four years now, been certified by an independent third-party certification agency for purchasing and processing only wood that meets accepted guidelines for environmentally responsible forest management.

For a smallish lumber mill to survive in modern-day Cook County requires a delicate touch. As Wes said following the 1981 fire, the mill must be right-sized for the available timber supply. Geography, history and politics have conspired to make Minnesota's Arrowhead a marginal timber producer. The good news is that lack of abundant timber keeps the big lumber companies from operating here, which creates an opening for the Hedstroms. They could not hope to compete with Potlatch, Weyerhaeuser and the other deep-pocket "big boys" for timber. Jack remarked recently, and only half in jest, that the Hedstrom mill may

have been more profitable through the Great Recession than it will be now that the economy is recovering—because sufficient timber was available at a price the Hedstroms could afford to pay.

But the other requirement is that the mill create products it can sell. This is where the Hedstroms excel, with Jack leading the charge until he retired and passed the baton to Jeff Johanns in 2013.

The Hedstroms' reasoning goes like this: We are a small mill with a limited supply of timber, and we have no access to low-cost rail shipping; everything must move by truck. So we cannot hope to compete with large mills producing "commodity lumber"—the 2 x 4s and similar lumber that form the bulk of the material sold at retail lumber yards. But we have a very flexible mill, and that allows us to tailor what we produce to meet the special lumber needs of specific customers. So we will focus on finding and serving niche markets. Yes, we will produce commodity lumber as a by-product of specialty manufacturing, but our bread and butter will be the niche products.

In the 1940s and '50s, Hedstrom Lumber Co. produced everything someone needed to build a home. That, Jack said, was because it was "customer-driven, and the customer was Andrew." In the 1990s, the Hedstroms came again to focus tightly on being customer-driven, and the customers were those who had needs for special wood products the Hedstroms could produce and were perhaps more willing to produce than large mills dedicated to commodity products.

Lumber mills tend to have a commodity culture, Jack said. "Many of them decide we're going to produce this and that, and then they instruct their sales force to go sell those products. We flipped that around. We decided we would find out what would sell, and then we would produce it. So sales drove how the mill operated and, to an extent, how timber procurement operated, rather than the reverse.

"But it can be difficult to overcome the commodity culture," Jack said. "Mills like to produce 2 x 4s and 2 x 6s; it's fast, it's efficient. When you tell a mill crew you need them to produce 3 x 5 pine blanks, they are resistant. That's where Merlyn Kiel was so important. He really understood what we were doing, and as sawmill foreman, he worked hard to ensure the mill produced what we could sell, along with the commodity lumber you inevitably get from every log after you take out the specialty products." The entire sawmill crew responded well to Kiel's direction.

"You need to be careful," Jack said. "Before you agree to a contract to provide a special product, you need to ensure you can sustain it. It's especially important that you know you will have the timber you need. I'm always telling Jeff (Johanns) to drive the log pile, see what you've got, and never, ever count on timber that is not in the pile. It's good to know what the procurement people say you are going to get, but never count on it until it is in the pile."

Once you've established your reputation as a customer-driven mill, Jack said, "people bring you ideas every week: Can you do this, can you do that? Before you agree to provide anything, there's a lot of due diligence. Of course you need to ensure you will be paid for the product, that the company you're producing for can keep its part of the bargain. But it's just as important that you ensure you can do the same: Do we have the timber for it, do the mill's capacity and its existing commitments allow for it, that sort of thing."

Ray Ruhanen doing the final inspection and grading before sorting.

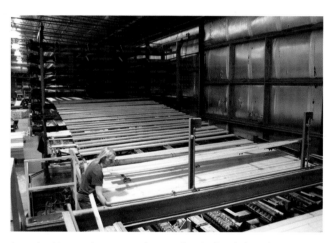

Jennifer Fenwick running the stacker behind the planer.

Howard looking at the wood boiler, which burns wood waste to make steam to dry the lumber and heat the whole plant. The mill has been thermal energy self-sufficient since 1975.

Jennifer Fenwick at the sorter in the planing mill.

As this customer-driven manufacturing took hold, the Hedstroms found themselves less and less focused on what had been their mainstay: retail. In the mid-1990s, they struggled with the same questions in their retail work that they faced at the mill: Was the retail operation right sized for the Cook County market, and was it producing a healthy revenue stream?

Once again, fire intervened to force the issue: In 1996, their large—perhaps too large—retail store and yard in Grand Marais burned to the ground in an arson fire. The Hedstroms sold the retail operation in order to, the company said, "focus on core business"—namely, keeping the lumber mill going strong by serving wholesale commodity and niche markets.

Also in 1996, the Hedstroms dipped deeper into the commodity lumber market when they purchased the Midwest Timber sawmill in Two Harbors. This was strictly a stud mill that produced 8-foot 2 x 4s and 1 x 4s, with an annual capacity of 12 million board feet, a little more than half the capacity of the Grand Marais mill.

One reason for the purchase, said Chris Hegg, finance manager for Hedstrom Lumber, was to eliminate a competitor for timber sales within the region the Hedstroms had marked off as critical for their survival.

"We're hemmed in by the big boys—Potlatch and others," Hegg said. "But they're not going to operate in our region; there's just not enough timber here to interest them." So the challenge for the Hedstroms is finding enough timber without venturing out of their home region and into direct competition with the larger companies that bid up the price. Purchasing the Two Harbors mill helped ensure that was possible.

The Hedstroms also calculated that the Two Harbors mill could, with substantial investment, be made efficient enough to add a stable source of revenue to the company's bottom line. And invest they did: A new kiln in 1998, an expansion and a sling sorter system

Lumber ready to go into the dry kiln.

in 1999, a sawdust and bark separator, and improvements to the debarker and gang edger in 2000.

Overall, however, as the 20th century and the first decade of third-generation leadership at Hedstrom Lumber came to a close, the company was in reasonably good shape. It had proven itself highly adaptive as it successfully survived a series of dramatic changes in the forest-products industry. While it wasn't rolling in revenue, it was staying afloat and providing a living for Hedstrom clan members and company employees.

None of the Hedstroms, however, was under any illusion that the turmoil was over. And they were right. Few industries are quicker to feel the effects of economic disruption than the forest-products industries, and for them, the 21st century so far has been notable mostly for the series of severe shocks that have struck the American and world economies.

It all began with the dot-com bubble collapse in 2000. As fortunes evaporated and layoffs rose, the American construction industries found their work disappearing at a rapid rate. And when there is no demand for new construction, there is no need for much commodity lumber.

The first victim was the Two Harbors plant. Despite a recent, costly upgrade at the plant, economic reality dictated that the Hedstroms move quickly to prevent collapse of the building market from pulling the entire company under. In late September 2000, Howard and Jack announced that the Two Harbors plant would temporarily close down.

"We are hoping this layoff will be short-term, but the outlook is quite dismal for the near future," Howard said at the time. "Production of lumber in North America has exceeded demand for many months now, and the economy is slowing down. Plus, we are heading into the time of year when construction slows down as well."

The sawmill area on a winter morning.

The sawmill log deck.

A load of logs arriving at the mill.

Howard's pessimism proved prophetic, and just a month later, the Hedstroms announced the Two Harbors mill was being closed for good.

Looking back, Jack finds a silver lining in the Two Harbors experiment. "Yes, we lost a million and a half dollars," he said. "But [in 1996] we also were talking about expanding the Grand Marais mill, and because we invested in Two Harbors, we didn't do that. So we came out of the whole thing with a mill in Grand Marais that was right-sized, very flexible and sustainable. If we had expanded it instead of buying the Two Harbors mill, the end result might have been a mill too large to sustain. We might not have survived."

They almost didn't survive anyway. The dot-com crash in 2000-2001 was followed by a series of economic slowdowns interspersed with small recoveries, culminating in the Great Recession that began in 2008. "We were slowly self-liquidating," Chris Hegg said. "We couldn't sell the timber we were producing, and we ran out of working capital."

The capital issue was solved thanks to The Lake Bank in Two Harbors, which provided the Hedstroms with a significant line of credit. "They did it, but it was well-papered," Hegg said. The IRRRB backed the loan. Bill Hansen of Sawbill Canoe Outfitters was sitting on the Northland Foundation board and got the foundation to back the credit line, too. The Small Business Administration also provided backing.

But a line of credit won't do you much good if you still can't sell the lumber you produce. As the economic slump continued into 2009, it became clear that the Hedstroms needed to call a time out and rethink their approach. Very reluctantly, they closed down the mill for two weeks and thought about how to proceed.

Hegg continued, "We knew we had to cut back the staff. But it was difficult to decide how to do that. The approach that finally worked was, we said, 'Here is how many people we can afford to employ. Now, how do we want to deploy them?' All of us took on many roles, including the office staff. I became head log scaler (the person who measures how much lumber a log will produce), for example.

"We cut the staff by about one-quarter. That meant we needed to purchase fewer logs, and of course we would produce less lumber. We went from a mill producing 25 million board feet and requiring 50,000 cords of wood per year to a mill producing 15 million board feet and requiring 30,000 cords per year.

The office staff from left: Bob Spry (20 years), Missy Smith (1 year), Chris Hegg (22 years), Jeff Johanns (1 year) and Howard Hedstrom (38 years).

The fourth generation from left: Jonathan Hedstrom (6 years), Kent Anderson (5 years) and Matt Anderson (13 years).

Wood procurement staff from left: Doug Magee (14 years), Jack Erickson (11 years), Kent Anderson and Jeff Elliott (9 years).

Maintenance: Matt Anderson and Cameron Kimball (14 years).

Filers: Rob Revier (16 years) and Burt Bockovich (20 years).

Sawmill graders from left: Ray Ruhanen (37 years), Ben Hadley (2 years) and Jeremy Jansen (5 years.)

Jennifer Fenwick (12 years).

Sticker plant from left: Mike Jansen (9 years), Jim Curtis (3 years) and Max Schlatter (1 year).

Planer mill crew from left: Ron Gervais (22 years), Joan Gervais (19 years), Al Norgaard (11 years), Roger Kloster (14 years), Robert Lutz (1 year) and Del Lutz (1 year).

"That downsizing was the best thing that has happened to us," Chris Hegg said. "I really think we came out of that with a sustainable model. We can continue to operate at this level well into the future, with the right leadership. We can secure the timber we need, and we can sell the lumber we produce.

"The leadership going forward won't be just family; it will be a mix of family and managers brought in from outside. That's clear. Jeff [Johanns] has replaced Jack, for example. But if we get the right people in the right places, this mill is well positioned to operate for decades to come."

Jack is less sanguine. Reflecting on the company's future from his winter retirement perch in Florida, he says the Hedstrom family has shifted and adapted and danced around difficulty for so long, and pulled so many rabbits out of the hat to get this far, that he's "not sure there are any rabbits left in any hats."

Howard leans more toward Chris' view: "There's not just room for a mill like ours," he said, "there's a need for it. The forests in our area are growing much faster than they are being harvested; the trees are getting bigger, and they are getting older. We should have an increasing amount of timber available for harvest far into the future."

Sawyers from left: Jon Buchheit (27 years), Terry Wilson (33 years), John Sheehy (11 years), Scott Houglum (20 years), Mike Kimball (23 years) and Ted Smith (27 years).

Glen Dahl (4 years), Adam Vonriedel (1 year), Roger Schoepflin (11 years) and Karl Schultz (1 year).

Yard man Josh Blegen (4 years).

Epilogue

Hedstrom Lumber Company has survived due to the family's determination, innovation and perseverance.

Thus ends this telling of the 100-year Hedstrom Lumber Co. saga. It is a saga foremost of two young Swedish immigrants—Andrew and Alma—working with great determination and vigor to create a life for their family in this wild and beautiful corner of Minnesota. How very close they came to failure at several points, but found somewhere, perhaps in each other, the wherewithal to push on, to not give up, to start over, again and again, to face down the demon—fire—which seemed to dog their steps.

It is easy, day-to-day, to lose sight of the grand sweep of the Hedstrom family's efforts to keep true to Andrew and Alma's legacy. As in any family, the Hedstroms have had their share of conflicts and disagreements, heartaches and disappointments. But if you raise your view from the trees in the Hedstrom forest to the forest itself, you see revealed a story of enormous courage, tenacity and humanity. That humanity perhaps was best captured by Bob Pratt. He has fond memories of the affection and care he was shown by the Hedstrom family, especially after he lost his father at a young age, saying, "the entire family was very nourishing, unconditionally positive to me."

Wayne Anderson and his son Kent best grasp the full grandeur of the enterprise—from the pile-of-junk Toftey mill through all the struggles to the present-day operation. Kent visiting a pile of sawdust at the old Sucker Lake camp pays an homage that is touching, deserved and encouraging. Undoubtedly, the second century of Hedstroms in the North Woods will be as filled with Swedish grit as the first.